EDWARD J. DENT

OPERA

ILLUSTRATED BY KAY AMBROSE

GREENWOOD PRESS, PUBLISHERS
WESTPORT, CONNECTICUT

Library of Congress Cataloging in Publication Data

Dent, Edward Joseph, 1876-1957.
    Opera.

    Reprint of the ed. published by Penguin
Books, Baltimore.
    Bibliography: p.
    1. Opera--History and criticism.
ML1700.D4607 1978   782.1   78-14482
ISBN 0-313-20563-9

First published 1940
Revised edition 1949

Reprinted with the permission of Penguin Books Ltd.

Reprinted in 1978 by Greenwood Press, Inc.
51 Riverside Avenue, Westport, CT 06880

Printed in the United States of America

10 9 8 7 6 5 4 3 2 1

PREFACE

THIS book is intended as an introduction to Opera for those who are just beginning, or perhaps have not yet begun, to take an interest in it. It is not a collection of synopses of opera plots; for at most opera performances nowadays a synopsis is printed on the programme. A few plots are here summarized, but only such as have either a special interest or such as illustrate particular phases in the history of Opera. I have treated the history of Opera in rough outline only, but I have tried to present it under various aspects, social, literary, dramatic and decorative, as well as purely musical.

I wish to express my thanks to Mr James Laver for helping me to choose various drawings and prints from the Victoria and Albert Museum as illustrations; to Sir Eric Maclagan for most kindly enabling me to have these photographed at a time when the Museum was inaccessible to the public, and also for permission to reproduce them here; to Mr Lawrence Haward, Curator of the City Art Gallery, Manchester, for further information and help; to the management of Sadler's Wells; to the photographer, Mr J. W. Debenham; to the various artists and to Mr J. B. Gordon, for the pictures illustrating modern productions at Sadler's Wells Theatre; and to Mr Paul Hirsch of Cambridge, for permission to reproduce various prints in his collection. Many of these prints and drawings of scenery at different periods have never been reproduced before. I must further thank Miss Kay Ambrose for making special simplified drawings of the Japanese revolving stage and of a design by Buontalenti of 1589, and also for her many charming and amusing decorations.

CAMBRIDGE,
February, 1940   2032503

POSTSCRIPT

In this revised edition I have tried to bring this book a little more up to date, especially as regards opera in England, where the changes of recent years have altered the whole operatic situation. Owing to the prevailing restrictions on foreign travel it has been impossible for me to see enough of opera in other countries to make any useful additions. I regret this most of all in the case of American opera and can only offer my apologies to my American readers for this unavoidable neglect. The only modern American opera which I have been able to see is Gershwin's Negro opera *Porgy and Bess,* performed by Danish opera-singers at Copenhagen, and in Danish; but fascinating and original as it is, I could not believe that it was representative, by itself, of the whole of America's contribution to musical drama.

1949

PHOTOGRAVURE PLATES

1. Bernardo Buontalenti (1536–1608), scene for an *intermezzo* in the entertainments given at Florence for the marriage of Ferdinand I de' Medici and Christina of Lorraine, 1589. This seems to be the scene for the second *intermezzo*, representing the singing-contest between the Pierides and the Muses. In the middle is Mount Helicon, with Pegasus standing on the top; lower down are six Hamadryads, and on the floor level a chorus of nymphs. The Pierides and Muses were in separate grottoes to right and left and are not seen in the drawing. This design gives a good idea of the scenery for the first Florentine operas, which grew out of the *intermezzi*. (Victoria and Albert Museum.)

2. Alfonso Parigi (d. 1656). This is probably a design for the scene representing the infernal regions in *Le Nozze degli Dei* (The Marriages of the Gods), an opera performed on a very lavish scale in honour of the marriage of Ferdinand II de' Medici and Vittoria Princess of Urbino, 1637. The music was by five composers whose names are not known. The design shows a large number of flying demons, etc.; probably many of these were dummies, though some may have been represented by human beings. There is an engraving of this scene showing the stage occupied by a ballet of centaurs, with flames bursting out in the wings. (Victoria and Albert Museum.)

3, 4. Ludovico Burnacini (1636–1707) worked for the imperial court at Vienna. These two scenes are taken from *La Monarchia Latina Trionfante* (The Triumph of the Holy Roman Empire), an immense allegorical opera, words by Nicola Minato, music by Antonio Draghi, with ballet music by J. H. Schmelzer, performed for the birth of the Archduke Joseph (afterwards Emperor Joseph I, 1705), heir to the Emperor Leopold I in 1667. In Scene 5, Peace, Prosperity and Religion take refuge from Bellona in a subterranean cavern. Earth commands the cavern to open and the classical gods are seen in the sky. The figures in the foreground are Prosperity, Religion (with the flame of faith on her head), Earth (with globe), and Peace (with olive-branch); above are Diana, Jupiter, Juno; Apollo, Venus, Mars, Cupid, Vulcan, with Mercury flying below. In Scene 16 we see the Elysian Fields, with a chorus of happy souls of Heroes, four of whom are raised to heaven. Above are Apollo, Diana, Mars and Venus; Ninus, Darius, Alexander the Great and Julius Caesar; below, flying, four figures representing the Four Monarchies, Assyria, Persia, Greece and Rome.

5. Guiseppe Galli da Bibiena (1696–1756) was descended from Giovanni

7

Maria Galli (1619–1665), a native of Bibiena in Tuscany, ancestor of several generations of theatrical architects, all of whom assumed the name Bibiena. Giuseppe worked mainly at Vienna and Berlin. This is a fine example of the palatial scenery used in all operas from about 1650 to 1750; the style has hardly yet died out, in spite of many changes of fashion, for it has always held the stage (for certain operas) in Italy, it has been consciously revived in Vienna, and it is the ancestor of the conventional 'palace set' still carried round by touring companies in England. (Victoria and Albert Museum.)

6. Design by Sir James Thornhill for *Arsinoe*, London, Theatre Royal, Drury Lane, 16 January 1706. (Victoria and Albert Museum.)

7. 8. Designs by C. F. Schinkel (1781–1847) for *The Magic Flute*, Berlin, Court Theatre, 18 January 1816. Plate 7 is for the scene in Act II in which the sleeping Pamina is approached by Monostatos; Plate 8 is the final scene. In front, disappearing, is the vault in which Monostatos and the Queen of Night are first seen; the starry sky above, with the stars arranged in characteristically formal lines, belongs to the first appearance of the Queen in Act I – a design which has been often reproduced; in the middle is the Temple of the Sun. The whole scene is shown in process of transformation. (Collection of Paul Hirsch, British Museum.)

9. Isaac Robert Cruikshank, caricature first published in 1818 and reissued in 1825; an amusing illustration of the social aspect of Italian Opera in London under the Regency. Title below: *A Dandy fainting or – An Exquisite in Fits. Opera – Scene a Private Box.* Inscriptions above: *I must draw the curtain or his screams will alarm the House. You have no fellow feeling my dear fellos, pray unlace the dear loves stays, and lay him on the Couch.* (2) *I am so frighten'd I can hardly stand!* (3) *Mind you don't soil the Dears Linnen.* (4) *I dread the consequence! that last Air of Signeur Nonballenas – has thrown him in such raptures, we must call in Doctor Clysterpipe immediately!* Inscription on the bottle: *Eau de Cologne.* Note, on the left, the boxes on the stage itself (such boxes existed in the Paris Opéra well into the present century), and the singer, wearing an abbreviated classical dress; on the right, the candles and refreshments, etc.

10. (*a*) The Wolf's Glen in *Der Freishütz*, lithograph on title-page of an English edition of the opera, 1824. (Collection of Paul Hirsch, British Museum.)

(*b*) Illustration by George Cruikshank, caricaturing the same scene, in the libretto of a 'travestie' of *Der Freischütz*, London, 1824. (Collection of Paul Hirsch, British Museum.)

11. Alessandro Sanquirico (1780–1847), design for *Amleto*, opera adapted from Shakespeare's *Hamlet*, words by Felice Romani, music

by Saverio Mercadante, Milan, Teatro La Scala, 1823. This scene represents the Tombs of the Kings of Denmark. (Victoria and Albert Museum.)

12. (*a*) First performance of *Lohengrin* at Weimar, 20 August 1850. *Leipziger Illustrierte Zeitung*. (Collection of Paul Hirsch, British Museum.)

(*b*) *Rigoletto*, Quartet in Act III. Lithograph on title-page of the vocal score, Milan, Ricordi, 1851. (Pendlebury Library, Cambridge.)

13. *Don Giovanni*, Sadler's Wells Theatre, Finale of Act I, 1938. Costumes and scenery by Charles Reading. Photography by J. W. Debenham.

14. (*a*) *Fidelio*, London, Sadler's Wells Theatre, 3 November 1937. Costumes and scenery by Bagnall Harris. Act II, Scene 1, Florestan in prison, Leonora and Rocco digging his grave. Photograph by J. W. Debenham.

(*b*) *Fra Diavolo*, London, Sadler's Wells Theatre, 1935. Design for Act III by Hans Strohbach. (Victoria and Albert Museum.)

15. *Il Trovatore*, London, Sadler's Wells Theatre, 1939. Costumes and scenery by Powell Lloyd. Act I, end of Scene 2. Photograph by J. W. Debenham.

16. *Hugh the Drover*, London, Sadler's Wells Theatre, 1937. Costumes and scenery by J. Procter-Gregg. End of Act I. The prizefight. Photograph by J. W. Debenham.

CONTENTS

Opera: An exotic and irrational entertainment.

Dr Johnson

CHAPTER ONE

THE APPROACH TO OPERA – SOCIAL CONDITIONS – POETRY AND MUSIC – THE FUNCTION OF MUSIC IN THE THEATRE

THE English tourist who returns from his first visit to Paris will probably remember some half-a-dozen outstanding 'sights' – the Eiffel Tower, the Arc de Triomphe, perhaps the Sacré-Coeur, and certainly the Opera. The Opera House is a thing that he cannot miss, even if he is in no great mood for sight-seeing; it is simply unavoidable. It occupies the most conspicuous site in the centre of modern Paris, and its mere bulk is gigantic; it is, in fact, the largest theatre in the world, as far as area is concerned. Some critics have said that it is grossly over-decorated and altogether an appalling monument of the worst nineteenth-century taste. It cost never mind how many millions; it took thirteen years to build, it employed innumerable sculptors and painters to decorate it with statues and frescoes which probably few people ever take the trouble to examine.

It was in that theatre that I first saw an opera – *Lohengrin* –

when I was only nineteen. Quite recently, after nearly half a century, I have had occasion to see several performances there and to spend many hours working in its quiet and dignified library; and the longer I looked at the frescoes and other decorations, all of which were thoroughly cleaned up for the exhibition of 1937, the more inwardly and continuously I was impressed with the thought that all this grandeur and magnificence, all this vast coordinated contribution of architects, sculptors, painters and engineers, had been assembled for the sole purpose of creating a house that should be worthy of music and the musical drama. We are accustomed to the idea that palaces and cathedrals should inspire a sense of wonder and awe in their beholders, but English people as a rule do not expect to derive such emotions from the sight of a theatre. We must go to other countries to find theatres, some ancient and venerable, some of comparatively recent erection, which stand in pride of place, proclaiming themselves centres of intellectual and artistic life for the communities which they serve. And it must be noted that almost every one of these historic theatres is an opera house; in some cities it may accommodate spoken drama as well, but its chief glory is and has always been the art of Music.

Foreigners often imagine that we have no opera in this country at all. In 1923 I heard an Italian musician, long resident in London, describing our musical culture to Maurice Ravel, who had just crossed the Channel for the first time. 'Music is completely dead in England now – the Italian opera has all come to an end.' That summed up the whole situation for the Italian gentleman. The history of opera in England – it will be sketched in a later chapter – makes curious reading. Its main characteristic is that from Sir William D'Avenant (1630) to Miss Lilian Baylis (1874–1937) it is a record of dogged perseverance on the part of a few enthusiasts, amateurs and visionaries.

After all, if opera in England is only a matter for amateurs and visionaries, why should we bother about it at all? What does it matter if the French and other foreigners think it important? Many of our most eminent leaders of music, both living and dead, have taken the view that opera is a form of music which ought not to be encouraged. If you cross-question

14

such people about their reactions to opera and try to make them think out the reasons why they disapprove of it, you will probably find them resentful and inclined to shut themselves up within the safe barrier of what they call 'good taste'. At the back of it all there is a certain remnant of puritanism, disguised today under the mask of socialism – *respectable* socialism, I need hardly say. As far back as the seventeenth century there were moralists in Italy, the home country of opera, who thought that the musical drama offered dangerous temptations; and songs were considered lascivious which the modern listener would find only quaint and formal. In the eighteenth century most opera singers were supposed to lead immoral lives, and in England it was something worse than that, for they were Italians and Papists, and therefore in all probability secret agents of the Pretender. The Victorians may have held similar opinions about the morals of the opera singers, but their sense of propriety was so refined that they preferred to ignore such things, and their sense of propriety also forbad them to criticize the pleasures of the aristocracy.

The moral disapproval of opera made itself felt more noticeably in the last half-century, when symphony concerts began to attract a popular public. Opera, it must be frankly admitted, had for centuries been a 'luxury of the aristocracy'. In all countries it had depended on kings and princes, or upon a wealthy nobility, for its financial support, and like all other forms of music and drama (apart from church music) it had been regarded as a source of pleasure. It is only since the days of Beethoven and Wagner that people have begun gradually to look upon music as a substitute for religion, and therefore to listen to symphonies and string quartets with a sort of devotional rapture. Even before the days of Beethoven German poets and philosophers had discovered a new idealism in pure instrumental music. The Germans of that period were indeed pioneers in symphonic music, but they were not very successful at opera so it was only natural for patriotic philosophers to point out that symphonic music was truly German, while opera was mainly French or Italian and therefore more or less reprehensible.

The great achievement of Wagner, as we shall see later, was to bring this religious spirit into the opera house; but in spite

15

of Bayreuth that spirit is none too firmly established, and in our day many musicians and music-lovers are beginning to react against the portentous solemnity with which the Wagnerian generation affected to listen to music. None the less, there are still many people in this country who take orchestral music very seriously, and who do not profess much interest in opera. Along with this ethical puritanism which I have mentioned there coexists, often in the very same people, a spirit of aesthetic snobbery, and it is a peculiar characteristic of English society that these two motives are often hardly distinguishable from each other. When a music-lover will not be content with anything short of what is absolutely perfect, are we to call him an ascetic or an epicure? We know the type that cannot bear to listen to a Beethoven symphony unless the finest of all existing orchestras is playing under the one and only *maestro*; and when this exclusive connoisseurship is applied to opera we may be sure that it will not lead to Sadler's Wells. There is, or was, one type of puritan epicure who never went inside any opera house except to hear the works of Gluck, Mozart or Beethoven; there are others, less puritanical and more exclusively epicurean, who will go only to Wagner. Others concentrate on being connoisseurs of voices, or of orchestras, scenery, or even of audiences; and you may be fairly sure that not one of these people takes any interest in operas as a complete whole or can form a sensible judgement on a new opera which he hears for the first time.

However, none of these people is likely to waste his money on this book, which is written mainly for those who are just beginning to go to opera, or perhaps have not yet begun. And why should they go to see operas? How many are there, I wonder, who come away from their first opera at Sadler's Wells as I did from *Lohengrin* in Paris, convinced that opera was to become the devotion of a lifetime? Or do they leave the theatre agreeing with Carlyle and Tolstoy that opera is just complete nonsense and a deplorable waste of time and money?

What makes opera difficult of access to the inexperienced listener is the fact that all operas are based on certain conventions not found in plays. These conventions are for the most part purely musical. There is first of all the convention by which the whole drama is sung instead of being spoken; and besides this there are often occasions when the whole action of the play is held up while a piece of music is sung. In the older operas we often hear words and sentences repeated over and over again, and one of the most ludicrous of conventions is that by which a character who ought to be in the greatest hurry to leave the stage remains in front of the footlights for several minutes informing us melodiously and with many reiterations that he 'must away' or 'can no longer stay'.

There is a historical reason for every one of these absurdities, though sometimes it is difficult to explain how such a convention developed without going into musical technicalities. In some operas the conventions are hardly noticed, because the beauty and fascination of the music itself holds the listener and makes him forget that the situation is contrary to common sense. At other times the convention becomes ludicrous or merely boring, and the reason generally is that the composer is imitating some older opera just because he thinks the device will be successful and profitable.

It is difficult to begin explaining these conventions and the reasons why they have come into being, because the ordinary operatic repertory – such as may be seen at Sadler's Wells, for instance, during the course of any winter season – includes works composed at very different times. It would be of little use for me to begin talking about *Faust*, let us say, as a typical opera, and explaining why the singers behave as they do, if my imaginary reader has just started his operatic experiences on *The Marriage of Figaro*. In a later chapter I must try to give a general survey of operatic history from the beginnings; but at this moment I am more concerned to induce my reader to go to Sadler's Wells for the first time. Perhaps he has just been there for the first time; that on the whole, is the more probable. He has seen *Faust*, or whatever his first opera may have been. I hope he has enjoyed it, but it is quite possible that he will say he has enjoyed some of it. At other moments he has been perhaps bewildered, irritated, or simply bored.

If I only knew which opera he had seen, I might be able to tell him something about it and suggest that he should go and see it again. Or I might, after hearing his criticisms on that particular opera, recommend him to give the theatre another chance by choosing a different opera that might please him better. Being unable to do this, it seems better that I should begin by asking what conventions are pretty well common to *all* operas which the reader is likely to see; how operas differ from plays, and how we are to find a way of either ignoring their absurdities or positively enjoying them.

The first and most obvious convention – or absurdity, if you like to call it so – is that the play is set to music. In some operas, such as *Faust*, there is some introductory music by the orchestra before the curtain rises, and after that the music goes on without interruption until the end of the first act. Much the same thing happens in every act. In other operas, however, the music is not continuous. There will be an overture for the orchestra, after which people applaud, and latecomers are admitted; then the band starts again, the curtain rises, and some sort of singing begins. It may be for one person, or it may be for two or more, possibly for a chorus; and then it will come to an end, and there will be a bit of dialogue spoken without music, leading to another musical item, or 'number', as such things are habitually called, from the fact that in the printed score of the opera each item is numbered consecutively for obvious convenience of reference at rehearsals.*

As a general rule, operas with spoken dialogue are comedies, and operas which are serious or tragic have music which is continuous all the way through. But there are exceptions, and from about the middle of the nineteenth century even comic operas quite often have continuous music. The fact is that composers have approached the problem of opera from two different angles. Are we to start by writing a straight play and then intersperse it with songs, or are we to start with the idea of continuous music all through, the spoken word being considered as something quite out of the question? The first opera ever composed, according to the orthodox history of music, started from the idea of continuous music. It is quite reasonable to begin the history of opera at this point, because al-

---

* The first score of a musical drama which was printed with consecutive numbers in this way was *La Rappresentazione dell' Anima e del Corpo* (*The Story of the Soul and the Body*), published at Rome in 1600; but the practice was not carried on (Handel's *Il Pastor Fido* (1712) is a rare exception), and it did not become general until nearly two hundred years later.

though the authors of *La Dafne* (Florence, 1594) had no idea what they were initiating, and certainly never called their work by the name of 'opera' in our modern sense of the word, still this seems to have been the first example (since the days of ancient Greece) of a play set to music all the way through with music composed by one and the same man with the intention of making it a complete artisic whole. Before that date there had been plays with incidental music, and plays in which large portions of the words were sung; but the probability is that such music as this was not composed by one man as a personal work of art, but just patched up and put together from any source that came handy.

We must obviously begin by considering this idea of singing a play instead of talking it. If it seems utterly ridiculous to us that a play should be sung, that means that our dramatic education has begun with modern comedies and farces in which the characters are ordinary people like ourselves. The author, even in plays which are intended to be poignantly emotional below the surface, purposely makes his dialogue as commonplace as possible, in order to convince us that his characters are real people and not stage heroes and heroines. And even if we care only about the most trivial kinds of music, we instinctively feel that ordinary phrases like 'have a drink' or 'what's the time?' are not suitable to be sung. All opera-goers will remember the moment in *Madame Butterfly* where the American Consul offers Lieutenant Pinkerton 'milk punch or whisky,' and as far back as 1656 D'Avenant, in *The Playhouse to Let*, makes an actor tease a musician about asking the time in recitative.

Yet music has been associated with drama from the earliest beginnings of the dramatic art. The most primitive forms of drama were religious festivals to which singing and dancing were indispensable. Music has always been an adjunct to religion, and in ancient times music has always been held to have magical powers. Music was supposed to put man in touch with the supernatural, as we see from such words as *charm, enchanter, incantation*, all of which are derived from singing. The function of music in drama is to lift us on to a higher emotional plane. I find it difficult to believe in my imaginary reader who has seen no plays except modern farces, unless he is quite an old gentleman by now, because in every school today children are taught to act Shakespeare. And everyone who has learned to act Shakespeare, or has seen Shakespeare acted, must inevitably have realized that poetry takes us into a new world. That new world is not a world of the impossible, a world which has no contact with the ordinary world in which we live every day; it is a world in which we feel our own personalities intensified. Everybody must have found characters in Shakespeare who represent for him what he feels or fears himself inwardly to be, the essential self of his dreams and aspirations.

This is one of the things which many people ascribe to the individual genius of William Shakespeare; they call it his humanity and universality. But it is really the product not of Shakespeare alone, but of poetry in general. We English people have been so long accustomed to sum up all dramatic poetry in the name of Shakespeare that we are apt to forget the historical fact that until comparatively recent times all spoken drama, tragic, comic or religious, was written in verse and not in prose.* That meant that the theatre, however trivial or vulgar the subject of the play might be, belonged to the realm of imagination, and not to the ordinary world of fact. It is obvious that music belongs entirely to the realm of imagination; and it is the function of music, in the theatre, to remove us altogether from the everyday world of fact. In the old-fashioned Victorian theatre it was a common practice for soft and sentimental music to be played by the orchestra in front as an accompaniment to some scene of deep emotion being acted (in spoken drama) on the stage; and at moments of horror the orchestra had to provide mysterious *tremolo* chords. Such things seem to us now merely ridiculous; but they have a long history behind them. These absurd bits of music are the poor relations of moments which in Wagner's operas may be overwhelming; and both Wagner and the Victorian band-leader inherited them from the same remote ancestors dating back to the time of Handel or earlier.

This way of utilizing music to create an atmosphere of mystery, whether in a play or in an opera, is what is generally called

* The earliest prose play is Ariosto's *La Cassaria* (1497) which the poet himself rewrote in verse twenty years later.

'romantic'. We shall see later on that it is mainly character-istic of a certain period of operatic history. And even in times when composers have made the instrumental background so important that it often seems to become the chief factor in the opera, they have still, however reluctantly, remembered that the characters on the stage have to sing and not speak. Supposing that we approached the theatre from the orchestral end, as many modern German composers seem to have done, and developed this 'background music' to such an extent that it went on continuously throughout the play, it would be use-less for the actors to speak at all. Their words simply would not be heard; their only chance is to sing, however unmelodi-ously.

In the earlier days of opera no composer would have dreamed of starting from the instrumental end. The characters on the stage were the presenters of the drama. It was the nor-mal and natural thing in the sixteenth century that drama should be in verse. Once we have accepted verse as a medium, music comes easy. There has been a long tradition of singing as a feature of drama, beginning (as far as the Christian era was concerned) with the liturgical dramas performed in churches and cathedrals from about the twelfth century on-wards. The music of some of these has come down to us, mainly from French sources; the words are mostly in Latin, but sometimes in the vernacular. Looking at these plays from the operatic, rather than from the religious, point of view, it is interesting to see that a comic element soon made its entry, and also that the authors and composers always seized the chance of emphasizing the 'eternal feminine' element. The Wise and Foolish Virgins were always a favourite subject, and Mary Magdalene sometimes becomes quite an operatic heroine.

The religious plays were sung from the first, because they were liturgical; they were developed out of the church ser-vice, acted by priests and choristers in the churches as part of the service itself. It was natural therefore that they should be sung to the same sort of chant as the rest of the liturgy. We know very little about the secular music of the Middle Ages, but we have enough evidence to show that it was in just the same style as the traditional music of the church, and that the church in quite early days (e.g. the thirteenth century) made use of music which to our ears sounds extremely lively and cheerful.

I do not want to weary the reader with a lecture on medieval drama; all I want to point out is that there is a continuous tradition of musical drama of some sort, sacred or secular, up to the time when opera, as we understand it, first came into being round about the year 1600, which is an easy date to remember. If the modern Englishman goes into Sadler's Wells and finds it absurd that people should be acting a play in music, it is because at some moment of history there has been a break in our own tradition. When we consider that Queen Elizabeth was a woman of exceptional intellect and artistic understanding, with not only the greatest poet and dramatist of all time in her employ, but also the greatest musician then living in Europe, William Byrd, it is indeed strange that this country should not have been the birthplace of opera.

Later on I propose to sketch the history of opera, first from the social and literary aspects, and then from the musical side; the reader who is bored by musical technicalities can skip that chapter and go on to the next. There will also be a separate section on opera in England, which will perhaps suggest reasons why the English people have not yet forced Parliament to subsidize a national opera house on the scale of Paris.

Perhaps, after all, it was superfluous to put forward historical reasons to justify the principle of setting a play to music; the average man needs no persuasion to make him enjoy musical comedy and revue, both of which could not exist without a large amount of music. It is no good for the serious-minded musician to pull a long face and preach a sermon on the deplorable frivolity of audiences and their invariable preference for bad music over good. If it is asked why people enjoy frivolous entertainments and will not go to operas, plenty of reasons could be found for showing that the public is guided merely by intelligence and common sense. They prefer to see on the stage young and physically attractive people who can act and dance as well as sing, instead of corpulent foreigners whose words are unintelligible even to those who know the language, and whose only idea of acting is to stand still and wave their arms. It is obvious that the promoters of musical comedies and revues take much more trouble over all that appeals to the eye, and it can sometimes be said that their orchestras could set an instructive example to the conductors of grand opera. But I dare not go further into these matters at this stage, for I should run the risk of frightening my readers away from opera for ever.

The man who goes to see an opera for the first time must take his chance, just as he must on his first visit to the playhouse or the cinema, except that in these later cases he will have been taken as a child to a play or film carefully chosen to suit his tender years. In Germany, at any rate in years gone by, children were often taken to the opera at an age when ours were taken to the pantomime, but English people of the present day are more likely to have to wait for their first opera until they are grown up. What suggestions can we make to them before the music begins, in the hope of helping them to enjoy the experience and wish to repeat it?

The lights go down and the orchestra begins to play. What is the object of that music? Why should not the curtain go up at once and the play begin? In a few modern operas – *Salome* and *Elektra,* by Richard Strauss – this does actually happen, but it does so mainly to startle the audience by violent breach with traditional custom. In the early days of opera the audience were summoned by a fanfare of trumpets, and so they were at the Wagner Theatre at Bayreuth. When opera became accessible to the general public, and perhaps even before, spectators would begin to assemble long before the time of beginning, and music would be an agreeable way of passing the time. But music before the play could always be of serious use in putting the audience into an appropriate frame of mind, provided they were willing to listen to it and not to talk all the time. It is very natural that people should want to talk in a theatre before the play begins, and most composers have recognized it. They wrote their overtures knowing quite well that conversation would only grow all the louder, and took very little trouble over them, little suspecting that two hundred years later learned Germans would find these flimsy affairs in libraries and try to turn them into solemn symphonies. Sometimes the composers made a desperate attempt to catch the attention of the audience by a pompous opening, and then hold that attention with music to which they could beat time; it was also useful, as well as economical, to introduce into the overture some of the later tunes which might well become popular. Even if the audience talked through them, they might stick in their subconscious minds. And occasionally composers took their introductions very seriously and set out to write something which would be an integral part of the opera, a prologue to explain it and set the emotional atmosphere of the whole work. If an introduction begins softly, it is a sign that we have reached a period when the composer can reasonably assume that his audience will listen to it in silence.

Whatever the character of the introduction, whether soft and mysterious, or noisy and frivolous, it has to tell us that we are going into a world of unreality, a world in which we are to forget the minor details of everyday life and surrender ourselves to the play of emotions which in everyday life we usually try to suppress or conceal, however deeply we may feel them. The great majority of operas deal with what we should roughly describe as 'classical' or 'romantic' subjects – stories from ancient Greek mythology, from remote ages and countries such as Egypt or Japan, from medieval history, or from any period that is not our own. Music seems to make these stories credible, or if not credible as records of actual fact, at any rate credible as expressions of human emotions. Verdi can make us believe in the story of *Aïda* but the play *Aïda* without the music would be impossible; it takes a Shakespeare to make us believe in *Antony and Cleopatra*, and even that is almost an opera.

There have been periods when composers have revolted against the romantic unreality of the operatic stage and have set out to be strictly realistic. At first this was possibly only in farcical comedy; but this farcical comedy itself – I speak of the days of the *Commedia dell'Arte* as set to music by some of the old Italian composers – was in its way an artistic convention and not a piece of real life, however real it might look by contrast with the heroic or mythological drama. Probably those comic scenes in opera, and those early comic operas about low life in Naples, were more realistic to their first audiences than they ever could be to us. If we ever revived them (*La Serva Padrona* of Pergolesi is about the only one ever seen nowadays), it would be the charm of the music that would hold a modern audience; they belong to the category of artificial comedy now and not to realism.

The same thing has happened in the case of a few modern operas. *La Traviata*, when it was first produced in 1853, was played in contemporary costume. It was a disastrous failure, and the usual reason alleged is that the consumptive heroine was sung by a very fat woman. Later on the opera was revived in some sort of historical costume, and soon became very popular; it was not until about 1904 that it was ever acted in the dresses of its own period, and by that time people had just begun to think that crinolines were romantic instead of merely frightful – so that *La Traviata*, historically a starting-point of realism, is now just as much of a romantic costume play as *Il Trovatore*.

An opera cannot be strictly realistic, because it depends on music for its expression, and music is intelligible as music only when it has a certain formality of structure. It is possible, especially in these days, to write continuous music in which the technical structure seems invisible, so that words can be in ordinary prose, and strict realism can have every chance; but the more realistic an opera is in that way the less attractive it proves to be to the general public.

In all operas, what really holds the audience is the beauty and expressiveness of the music. The cultivated concert-goer must be told to take these words in a broad human sense, and to admit beauty in such a tune as 'I dreamt that I dwelt in marble halls'. He must forget his associations of that tune with the red-nosed cornet player in a back street, and imagine the song sung under perfect conditions of voice and style, and of physical appearance, too. Even under ordinary conditions that song holds a popular audience.

Whatever it is that has filled countless theatres to listen to *The Bohemian Girl*, it is certainly not realism. It is hard to imagine in these days that anybody could go to *The Bohemian Girl* and feel that they were seeing their ideal selves on the stage, as they still might do for almost any play of Shakespeare, but it is not inconceivable that people felt like that fifty years ago or more. The success of *La Bohème* (as an

Italian composer once pointed out to me) has been due to the fact that every girl in the gallery can think of herself as Mimi, but the very unreal realism of that opera is a small matter compared to the attractiveness, and the continuous attractiveness, of the music. How long that will last we cannot prophesy. We look back to such an opera as *Fidelio*, an undoubted masterpiece by a man who is still acknowledged by most people as the greatest composer who ever lived, and wonder why certain parts of it are dull. Were they dull when they were first written? We find them dull now because we are conscious of them as formalities of their period. But we cannot cut them out of the music just by skipping a page here and there; if we try to do that we shall find that they were essential to Beethoven's thought, and that the music sounds wrong without them. In that case, it must be our fault for not understanding them, and experience shows that these dull places can be made stirring if they are played and sung with sufficient faith and intensity.

Here we see something of the troubles that are likely to confront the incipient opera-goer. It does not much matter where he sees his operas; to witness the perfect performance of a perfect work of art is an experience for which we might thank our stars if we could achieve it once in a lifetime.

Some opera-goers want to hear voices (and to think themselves connoisseurs) and some want to hear orchestras. A German friend of mine was once commissioned to write a book about opera. 'I shall begin with a chapter on the orchestra,' he said, 'for that is the most important thing.' And we never could enjoy an opera together, for he always wanted to sit in a side box where he could see the conductor in profile and all the players; he thought me very innocent for wanting to look at the stage. The more I frequent opera, the more keenly I am interested in the work itself and its presentation as a whole, and the more indifferent I become to its individual parts. But although I should always prefer not to see the orchestra at all, and certainly not the conductor, whose distracting and self-exhibiting gestures are the public nuisance of almost all opera houses, I want to see the whole stage, hear the singers and see them, too, and also understand the words. It is one of the oddities of opera in this country that many people (especially of the older generation) will say that they prefer not to know what an opera is about, for all opera plots are so silly that they think they can make up better stories for themselves out of their enjoyment of the music. We are still haunted by Dr Johnson's famous definition of opera; and hopeless – indeed, blasphemous – as it may seem to challenge any opinion of that great incarnation of the English character, the object of this book is to invite you to put a new interpretation upon it.

CHAPTER TWO

THE BEGINNINGS OF OPERA — MONTEVERDI — VENETIAN OPERA — LULLY AND RAMEAU — COMIC OPERA

WHAT astonished me most, the first time that I entered Covent Garden Theatre, was the fact that there were boxes all round the house; and when I first went to Italy I was still more surprised to find that in almost every theatre there were boxes all the way round and all the way up until one reached the gallery. The fact is that the majority of Italian theatres are very old, built in the eighteenth or early nineteenth century; some were burned down and rebuilt in the middle of the nineteenth century, like the Fenice at Venice, but the old plan was preserved. Covent Garden (built in 1856) copied the Italian system, although for this country it was long out of date; but the box plan remained traditional for opera, because opera was always felt to be something different from the ordinary drama, not only on the stage, but in all its surroundings and accessories. A musician well known in the social world said to me soon after the opening of Sadler's Wells in 1931, 'You can't make an opera house out of Sadler's Wells; there are no boxes; people simply won't come.'

Shocking as it may be to those who preach the doctrine of 'music for the people,' it is a historical fact that opera, ever since it first came into being, has flourished most conspicuously when it was under the patronage of a court and an aristocracy. That is why it presents so difficult an economic problem at the present day, for modern monarchs have little time to be musical, or even to pretend to an interest in music for the sake of duty; and aristocracies, when they are well off, have discovered various other distractions. There still survives a vague tradition that opera ought to be an affair of full dress and diamond tiaras, though elderly opera-goers talk regretfully of the days of Queen Alexandra, and in 1830 it was remarked that the opera was no longer as smart as it had been in the Regency.

The first operas ever put together were the creation of a small set of aristocratic intellectuals in what was then the most intellectual city of Europe – Florence. For more than a hundred years North Italy had been the centre of all artistic culture – architecture, sculpture, painting, poetry and music, all encouraged and protected by small courts and aristocracies. In music, and in drama as well, there was a wide gulf between the art of the 'intellectuals' and that of 'the people', just as there is at the present day. Popular drama was represented by the Comedy of Masks, which no doubt the aristocracy enjoyed as much as anyone else; and intellectual drama by the learned comedies of Ariosto and others, appealing only to a classically educated audience. These comedies were generally accompanied by incidental music; music, that is to say, in the shape of madrigals between the acts, not integral to the play. And there were other entertainments, more in the nature of masques (indeed, most of the ideas in our own Jacobean masques are borrowed from Florentine originals), in which drama was more an excuse for pageantry, dancing, scenic architecture and music. One of the landmarks in the history

29

of these spectacles is the *Orfeo* of Angelo Poliziano, produced at Mantua in 1472 with scenery painted by Raphael. About the music nothing is known at all, but the structure of the poem shows that a great deal of it must have been sung. The interest of Poliziano's *Orfeo* lies in the fact that it was the first attempt to adapt the methods of the medieval morality plays to a subject from classical mythology in the spirit of the Renaissance.

All these semi-dramatic and musical spectacles in the following century were isolated single performances, produced in theatres specially erected for the occasion. At the present day the word 'opera' suggests a permanent theatre of imposing dimensions in which a different opera is performed every night for the greater part of the year. In early times there were no permanent theatres and no operatic repertory, for the simple reason that very few operas had been composed at all. The production of such a work, as was the case with the English masques, entailed enormous expense, and could only be undertaken to celebrate some important occasion such as a princely wedding. The undisguised 'intellectualism' of such performances would limit their appreciation to a comparatively small circle, although, naturally, there were plenty of people, as we know from contemporary literature, whc enjoyed the show as an expensive spectacle and went there to be seen as well as to see.

The earliest opera of which we have the music complete is Peri's *Euridice* (Florence, 1600). The idea of the authors was to revive the musical declamation of ancient Greek tragedy; the spirit behind the production, one might say, must have been rather like that which first induced people at Oxford and Cambridge to act plays in Greek about eighty years ago. Only this version of the Orpheus legend was not in Greek, nor even a translation from Greek; it was an original poem in Italian by Ottavio Rinuccini. The first performance must have been what we should call a very small affair, and it is difficult for us to believe that the audience was not inclined to find it tedious; but we must not judge it by the music alone. The original audience might well have been thrilled by the poetry itself, for Rinuccini was a real poet, no mere 'hack librettist', for such people did not exist in those days. As opera – to use our name for it – was making its first appearance on any stage, the audience had no standards by which to judge it, and quite probably they never expected the music to be more than a very subordinate item. Peri, whether from amateurish incompetence or from self-imposed asceticism, ignored most of the technical devices current in the music of his day, such as are illustrated in the madrigals of Luca Marenzio; it is evident, both from the music and from what contemporaries said about it, that the declamation of the words came before everything.

Here the ordinary man of today may reasonably ask why the words should have sounded any better in this tedious musical declamation, accompanied by chords on lutes and other instruments, than recited in the ordinary way. It can only be answered that in those days people were intensely interested in this problem of musical recitation, both in Italy and in England. The method was very soon seized upon by the English composers, its chief exponent being Milton's friend Henry Lawes; and the curious thing is that it survived well into the period of the Restoration, for Pepys, who is a very good example of the cultured amateur musician, was always fascinated by it, and got one of his teachers to write down a musical setting of Hamlet's soliloquy, 'To be, or not to be', which was supposed to reproduce as nearly as possible the declamation of the famous actor Betterton.

In our day we have made so wide a separation between poetry and music that music-lovers find any sort of declamatory singing dull and unmusical, while poetry-lovers think a 'sing-song' style of recitation detestable. But it is a fact that many poets of recent times – Tennyson among others – recited their own poems in a sort of chant very disconcerting to their musical listeners, as Hubert Parry said of Tennyson; and it seems probable that on the stage of the seventeenth century there was a borderland between speaking and singing. Further, it must be remembered that as opera was in its infancy, a long time had to elapse before any standard style of operatic singing was evolved and practised.

How uncertain people were at this time as to what they were aiming at is shown by other contemporary experiments in musical drama. In 1597 Orazio Vecchi, a canon of the

31

cathedral of Modena, published his *Amfiparnaso*, modestly calling it 'the lower slopes of Parnassus', which was a series of fourteen madrigals illustrating the Comedy of Masks. The words of the Prologue (sung) made it absolutely certain that he never intended it to be acted, and there is no reason why the little woodcuts of actors in the printed part-books should be anything more than illustrations like those of a novel. It is an extremely spirited and humorous work; and it has been revived in Italy, and in England, too, with the story acted in dumb show, sometimes by puppets, while a chorus sing the madrigals; this makes it more intelligible to a modern audience, but it is certainly not what the composer expected.

Another interesting experiment was the *Rappresentazione dell' Anima e del Corpo* (*The Story of the Soul and the Body*) set to music by Emilio de' Cavalieri at Rome in 1600. Cavalieri had lived many years in Florence and must have been in close contact with what we may call 'the opera circle'. This work is a morality play, rather like *Everyman*, pieced together from earlier sources, and set to simple music with hymns to be sung between the episodes. There are elaborate directions for performance, and it was certainly meant to be acted in costume, with dancing as well, but in its general spirit it is a 'devotion' rather than an opera. (Histories of music always call it the first oratorio, but this is misleading.)

The man of genius who saw what opera might become was Claudio Monteverdi, whose *Orfeo* was produced at Mantua in 1607; it was followed by *Arianna* (the classical story of Bacchus and Ariadne) in 1608. Most of the music to *Arianna* is lost, but *Orfeo* has survived complete, and has had many revivals recently, some of them in rather garbled versions. The most modest production, and at the same time the most scholarly and understanding, was that conducted by Mr J. A. Westrup at Oxford some years ago.

Monteverdi has gone down to posterity as the prototype of the daring revolutionary in music. He was nothing of the sort. He was a highly accomplished composer of music both sacred and secular, with every orthodox technique at his fingers' ends. He has been credited with various daring innovations, but it is no disparagement to his originality to say that most of them had been made years before. But he must have been a man of wonderful courage and organizing ability as well as a visionary, for he seems to have known exactly what he wanted to do and how to carry it out. He saw that this new form of entertainment could make use of every resource that was available. Peri's opera aims at being ascetic and results in being anaemic; all the way through it seems to be refusing to go too far, from a spirit of self-conscious good taste. Monteverdi had behind him the experience of the dramatic madrigal, in which passionate emotion had been expressed with almost terrifying intensity. He evidently had the vision of opera such as Wagner claimed to have conceived, a form of art in which all the arts were to converge on a single purpose.

For some time opera remained the plaything of princes, and it soon came down from its lofty pedestal of mythology and began to make a more obvious appeal to people who were not in the 'intellectual smart set'. Comic elements were introduced, and sometimes very clearly and successfully. In 1637 the first public opera house was opened at Venice. Venice was ruled not by a court, but by an oligarchy of wealthy families; it was the city of intellectual freedom, and also the city of pleasure, like Monte Carlo in our days. Ben Jonson's play, *Volpone*, shows the sort of English tourists who went there, and you may meet their modern equivalents there still. Some astute business men saw that the opera was going to attract strangers, and in a very short time opera was such a prosperous undertaking that several theatres had been opened at which opera was performed. Most of them belonged to the well-known Venetian noble families such as the Grimanis and the Mocenigos.

Opera was still carried on elsewhere in the old princely fashion, with occasional performances to celebrate weddings and so forth, but the Venetian commercial opera soon brought about a certain standardization, both in the general musical and literary form of opera and in all its accessories. Scenery still played a most sumptuous part, and as the seventeenth century was a great age of engineering, stage machinery was developed to an incredible pitch of ingenuity and skill. Hundreds of designs and diagrams have come down to us, and it is interesting to note that in the general history of the theatre opera, and not drama, takes the lead in every branch of theatrical architecture. Baroque architecture is in fact the art of the theatre, and the stage offered an artist far more fantastic opportunities for his imagination than any prince or nobleman could afford to commission in solid brick and stone.

The Venetian operas – and they were the standard type for opera everywhere – were extravagant in every sense. The librettos generally dealt with heroes and heroines of antiquity or of the Roman Empire, early and late, rather than with gods and goddesses, though these sometimes made their appearance in a prologue. Audiences did not want scholarly poetry, but stories of human passion and intrigue. They also wanted grandeur, as in the classical French theatres. There was no idea of conforming to the 'unities' of time and place when transformation scenes were one of the main attractions, but generally speaking the characters had to be on the heroic plane. And, as in the Shakespearean theatre, there was plenty of comic relief. Outside Venice the opera in course of time spread to Bologna, Rome and Naples; it crossed the Alps to Paris and Vienna, spreading eventually to the smaller courts of Germany and to Hamburg, the Venice of the North. Hamburg, as one might expect, was the first German town to run commercial opera on Venetian lines, as far as it could manage it. Vienna saw in the opera a magnificent opportunity for glorifying the house of Hapsburg. Italian architects, poets and musicians were imported regardless of expense to create such monstrous spectacles as *La Monarchia Latina Trionfante*, the music for which was written by Antonio Draghi (1667). Draghi, in the course of some thirty years spent in Vienna, wrote a large number of operas and similar entertainments for the court, remembered now only by the scenic designs of his collaborator Burnacini.

The French were more sceptical about the new entertainment. There was a political background to Cardinal Mazarin's attempts to establish Italian opera in Paris during the minority of Louis XIV, who had succeeded to the throne at the age of six. French musicians were naturally jealous of the Italians, and they found Italian music too violent and hysterical for their taste. France had its own musical traditions, and probably Frenchmen had not entirely forgotten that Italy had got

34

most of her music from French and Netherlandish composers a hundred years before. Cavalli, the creator of Venetian opera from 1637 onwards, was invited to Paris in 1660, and his opera *Serse* was produced there with elaborate scenes and machines invented by the Italian stage architect Torelli, but that was the end of Italian opera in Paris for a long time. The French wanted an opera of their own, and it was another Italian who established it for them.

Giovanni Battista Lulli (1632–87), generally known as Lully, was brought from Italy to Paris as a boy. He began his career as a playmate of Louis XIV and made his way as a dancer and singer. Later he collaborated with Molière, providing dances and other music for his comedies, and in 1672 he composed a French opera, *Les Fêtes de l'Amour et de Bacchus*. Lully was a great organizer and constructor rather than a great composer; his music is often dry and formal. But although he never learned to speak French well enough to appear in a French part on the stage, he created, or at any rate standardized, the traditional style of French recitative, which is quite different from the Italian. Lully's operas, like those of Draghi at Vienna, were planned to glorify the reigning monarch, and every one has a prologue in which some divinity descends from Heaven to inform the audience that Louis is the greatest king who ever lived. Fortunately he had a distinguished poet as a collaborator, and Quinault's librettos helped to give these operas a wonderful sense of dignity and style.

Towards the end of the seventeenth century Naples became the chief centre of Italian opera. By this time French and Spanish influences had begun to make themselves felt in the construction of librettos. The Spanish influence seems to have been confined to certain operas on a small scale belonging to the last years of the seventeenth century and almost comic in character; the French influence, derived from Corneille and Racine, affected the more serious heroic type. Apostole Zeno, who was court poet to the Emperor Charles VI, wrote a great many librettos, originally for Italian composers at the Court of Vienna, though they were often re-set, with or without alterations, by later musicians elsewhere. Zeno's main object was to reduce the comic element; instead of appearing all over the play at the most unexpected moments, as they had done in the rather chaotic Venetian operas, the comic characters were allotted separate scenes of their own, generally at or near the ends of the acts. Zeno also established the tradition of three acts, in preference to the five of the earlier operas. These changes may seem of little importance, but they all made for a stiffer formalization of the Italian opera, and it is just this conventional formality which makes opera of those days so unsympathetic to the modern mind, at any rate in England.

We English are accustomed to regard Shakespeare as the standard to which all serious drama of the poetic type must be referred. Shakespeare is the ideal poet and dramatist; he can do no wrong. We cannot understand the French attitude towards him, as exemplified by Voltaire, because we have never bothered our heads about the 'unities', and many English people do not even know what they are. Italian opera had started from Greek ideals, but it very soon abandoned them, and took no notice of the unities, any more than the Shakespearean theatre did. But it was only natural that Italian poets should be affected by the principles of the French theatre during the century of Corneille, Racine and Molière; such a triad of genius could only be paralleled by Dante, Petrarch and Boccaccio, or in a later age by Haydn, Mozart and Beethoven. Apostolo Zeno was followed by Pietro Metastasio, also laureate to the imperial court in his later years; he counts as one of Italy's great poets, although he devoted himself almost entirely to writing opera librettos and other verses for musical setting. Mestasio's musical dramas were so much admired that they were set over and over again by every composer of the time; there was no copyright in such things, and even if the first setting or performance brought some fee to the poet, the subsequent ones seem to have been beyond his control.

Metastasio's librettos are even more formal than Zeno's, if only for the reason that he is a better poet, with a more elegant choice of language and a more exquisite chivalry of conduct. The comic characters he eliminated altogether, though he was by no means without a sense of humour and wrote some definitely comic librettos as well. Plots were still based on legends of antiquity or on episodes from medieval history; Zeno, it may be noted, wrote a libretto on Hamlet, derived not from Shakespeare, but from Saxo Grammaticus, the source utilized by him. All operas had to have a happy end, in which the principal characters paired off, unless they were married already. Plots are curiously like those of the typical Victorian melodrama; and the Victorian melodrama, as we shall see later on, is lineally descended from the opera. That is in fact the reason why it was called melodrama, for *melodramma* is the classic Italian name for what we call opera. The name *opera* had already come into colloquial use by 1644, for John Evelyn notes it in his diary at Rome; but on the title pages of scores and librettos an opera is generally called *melodramma* or *dramma per musica*. The French name was usually *tragédie lyrique*; I doubt if the word *opera* appears on any Italian title-page before 1800, although it certainly was used in England as far back as 1656, and was the regular name for musical dramas in England all through the periods of Locke, Purcell and Handel.

Italian opera of the Metastasian type that prevailed for (roughly speaking) the first half of the eighteenth century was so remote from any sort of opera current on the stage of today that modern opera-goers can hardly conceive how it was tolerable. It has returned to life in recent years, at any rate in occasional performances, owing to a revival of interest in the operas of Handel. Metastasio's dramas are written in exquisite Italian, but are all very much alike. Whatever the story, even when on one occasion he laid the scene in a quite imaginary China, there is generally the same sort of noble hero, suffering heroine, and usurping villain, with a subsidiary pair of lovers as well. The opera consists almost entirely of solo songs, separated by recitatives; allowing for their formalities, the recitatives are often very dramatic, and the songs, when set to music by a great master, could be supremely beautiful and expressive. The number and order of the songs were strictly regulated; each principal character had to have so many, in various styles, and the secondary characters fewer, perhaps two each. At the end of a song the singer invariably left the stage; this had not been the rule in the earlier Venetian operas, but Metastasio and Zeno were rigid on this point. The song was supposed to sum up the emotional situation. The complexity of the plots was due to the exaggerated chivalry of the characters, and this too accounted for the formality of language in which all emotions had to be expressed. All Metastasio's librettos were written for court festivities, so that all his monarchs had to be made incredibly magnanimous. Some were intended for amateur performance by the archdukes and archduchesses. The reason why *L'Eros Cinese* was Chinese was simply because the archduchesses could not possibly exhibit their legs in male parts; as Chinese however they could wear long dresses. Occasionally two persons were allowed to sing a duet; but any larger ensemble was almost unheard of. Alessandro Scarlatti invented the 'ensemble of perplexity', which is a song divided among three or four characters, all saying that they cannot think what to do in this terrible situation; but it was a long time before composers made a regular practice of this device. The important thing to note is that everything dramatic, and all the explanations that were necessary to bring the story to a happy end, were made in plain recitative with the minimum of accompaniment – little more than natural speech, in fact. After all difficulties had been smoothed out, there was a short finale sung by all the principals together, generally to something like a dance tune. There were hardly ever any choruses at all; sometimes a body of soldiers would shout 'Death to the tyrant!' or similar exclamations, which could easily be learned by ear by any Italian supers. In a few of Handel's London operas there are longer choruses and also ballets, but these are exceptional. In Italy the ballets were quite separate from the opera and the music was by some other composer, generally French.

Two situations arose from the fact that Metastasio's plays were set by dozens of different composers. In Italy the audiences must soon have known the plays by heart. In Germany and England the regular *habitués* must at least have known the beginnings of the songs by heart, and must have taken very little interest in the recitatives which they did not understand. The Italian opera became just a concert in costume. And while the costumes were not very different from those worn by the audience, especially the dresses of the ladies, the scenery represented the same sort of palaces and gardens, even the same sort of sham ruins, that the wealthy subscribers were building and laying out for themselves.

At Naples, the headquarters of the operatic industry, a new type of opera was being evolved early in the eighteenth century – comic opera, or, as its authors called it, 'comedy in music'. Its characters were ordinary people, often people of humble life, talking the Neapolitan dialect, and singing the songs of the streets and the sea-shore. The performers at the little theatre which specialized in this form of entertainment did not profess to be 'singers'; they were described as comedians, but probably every man and woman in Naples could sing, and in a very short time the comic opera was firmly established and the most serious composers of the day contributed their share to it in the intervals of writing court operas and church music.

Foreigners went to see these amusing little operas and wrote home about them; in 1740 a Neapolitan company appeared in London. The fashion spread to Bologna and Venice; by the middle of the century Venice was rapidly becoming the main source of supply, though Naples went on being active into the nineteenth century. In 1752 a Neapolitan company went to Paris; Jean-Jacques Rousseau, himself an amateur composer, proclaimed that no music was worth listening to unless it came from Naples. French opera at that moment was represented by Rameau, who continued and developed the stiff and formal opera of Lully. Rameau was perhaps the greatest musician that France has ever produced, and he was French by birth and education, which is a rare phenomenon in the history of French music. The great composers of French opera have been mostly foreigners; but so strong is the influence of French culture that their works for the French stage have been completely French in style, and the qualities which have handed down their names to the admiration of posterity have been those which they acquired from France.

Rameau's operas were quite different in construction from those of the Italians, although they dealt with much the same subjects in the same spirit of courtly formality. The French had always preferred declamation to singing, and France cultivated two things which Italy practically ignored in the theatre, the chorus and the ballet. Rameau, too, is the first operatic composer who habitually used the orchestra for descriptive purposes, for the representation of storms and rolling seas. We can find the beginnings of these devices in Lully, and also in the English composers Locke and Purcell, but the Italians, in spite of their having been the great inventors of stage machinery, seem to have utterly ignored the possibility of picturing their visual effects in music. The Italian mind was always concentrated on singing; the French were never remarkable for their voices, and foreign critics from Italy and England were unanimous in declaring that French music and French opera made the most excruciating noise that ever assailed human ears.

The visit of the Neapolitan comedians showed the French a new aspect of dramatic music. In all probability the Italian singers of this troupe were by no means great artists with incomparable voices; and the singers at the French opera, whatever the Italians thought of them, were people who carried on a tradition of immense nobility and dignity. It may be doubted whether the Italian orchestra was any better than the French; what must be quite certain from the mere study of the scores is that whereas Rameau's instrumental music was sonorous and elaborated with the greatest care, the Italian comic operas of that time were all of the flimsiest possible type, written in a hurry with the minimum of workmanship, and trusting to the harpsichordist to provide most of the support for the eccentricities of the singers. But the Italians won the 'war of the *bouffons*', as it was called – a war mainly of journalists, as one might imagine – because their little operas were human and alive, while Rameau was an ageing man, a supreme master, but master of a dying tradition.

The Italians conquered Paris, but Paris, as always, absorbed them and they ceased to be Italian. The second half of the eighteenth century shows the triumph of comic opera over serious musical drama. In all countries where opera was cultivated, the serious opera, whether French or Italian, had been associated with some sort of a princely court. We are accustomed nowadays to think of opera as a matter rather of routine; whether it is in Paris, Dresden, Rome or Sadler's Wells, we expect to find a theatre giving opera more or less every night of the week for several months on end, and performing a different work each night. But it must be remembered that this permanent repertory system took a very long time to establish, and although it is difficult to say exactly when and where it came into being, we may say roughly that before about 1800 – a round figure that we can connect with the age of Napoleon – serious opera is mainly an *occasional* entertainment, that is, a ceremonial function to celebrate a particular festivity. It can easily be understood that the transition from this system to the public repertory system was gradual; but our own short Covent Garden season of international opera used to be an annual reminder of what opera signified in a social sense two hundred years ago. It was natural, therefore, that opera on the grand scale should be hedged in by privileges and monopolies, in order to prevent the success of rival undertakings; and this accounts for the long period during which there were two sorts of opera in existence, the formal ceremonious opera of the court, and, at the opposite end of the social scale, the comic opera of the people.

In Italy and France both types of opera had this much in common, that the language of both was the language of the country, but in Germany and England, as well as in Denmark, Sweden and Russia, where opera gradually began to make its way during the eighteenth century, serious opera was always in Italian. Opera had in fact become a great Italian industry, and it was the ambition of every Italian composer and singer to get himself attached to some foreign court. It was also the ambition of every northern composer to travel to Italy for his musical education, if he could possibly find a patron to pay for it, and those who had to remain at home were bitterly jealous of the Italians and of their fellow-countrymen who adopted Italian methods and sometimes Italian names as well.

It is necessary to insist very strongly on this wide social gulf between serious and comic opera – a gulf all the greater in the northern countries and in Central Europe – because our modern repertory makes no very great distinction between the two classes. Paris has always separated *grand opéra* from *opéra-comique*, but the distinction has come to be mainly one of size. The Opéra-Comique admits spoken dialogue, the Opéra does not; that is the official distinction, but it is obvious that spoken dialogue can be conveniently heard only in a smallish house. In a few of the German cities there were two court theatres, large and small, and operas and plays were both allotted to them according to size and character. But just as the dramatic repertory of the court playhouse included both tragedy and comedy, so the court or state opera was open to both Meyerbeer's magnificence and the wit of Auber, even in the reign of Emperor William II.

In the middle of the eighteenth century this was not the case; comic opera was still in a definitely inferior position, even in Italy. That does not mean that it was not enjoyed by the wealthier classes; on the contrary, it was frequented by the same sort of people who go to revues and musical comedies at the present day, although its development was for a long time hampered by the restrictions governing the non-privileged theatres. It was not until after the Revolution that these restrictions were removed in France, but none the less a French tradition of style was gradually built up, and it is historically important because it is the basis not only of subsequent comic opera but also of all that we can call romantic opera. At the present day we are accustomed to see all sorts of periods put on the stage in opera; and to the average English opera-goer the term 'opera' or 'grand opera' covers a very wide range. Up to the time of the French Revolution the subjects of serious opera were almost exclusively restricted to the days of ancient Greece and the Roman Empire, with a certain extension towards the Middle Ages in stories taken from the epic poems of Ariosto and Tasso. Comic opera, on the other hand, seems to have confined itself almost entirely to contemporary life, both in France and in Italy, and it is only towards the end of the century that comic opera begins to deal with medieval subjects. It is necessary to emphasize this, because when we perform an eighteenth-century comic opera now we see it as a period piece, with all the charm of quaint romance, whereas originally it was a play of modern life in modern dress.

CHAPTER THREE

GLUCK –
BEGINNINGS OF GERMAN OPERA –
MOZART

WE now come to one of the outstanding figures in the history
of opera, Christoph Willibald Gluck (1714–87), and at the
same time we reach the oldest operas that are now included
in the general standard repertory. Operas by older composers
are sometimes revived, and occasionally they meet with an
unexpected success; but Gluck's – and only a very few of
these – are the earliest which still keep the regular professional stage.

Gluck was born in Bavaria, at a village called Erasbach,
about half-way between Nürnberg and Regensburg; a good
part of his life was passed in Vienna, where he died, so that
German writers have always considered him as one of the
great German masters. Indeed, it has been the tendency of
German critics to make out that all operatic history is summed
up in the five German names of Gluck, Mozart, Beethoven,
Weber and Wagner. Nothing could be more misleading, as we
shall see in the course of this book. Gluck, like Handel, was
an international eclectic, and the same might be said of
Mozart. Even Weber's music can be analysed into components
that are French and Italian as well as German, and there are
things in Wagner's operas which betray the fact that in his
younger days the German operatic repertory was far less
German than French.

The name Gluck is more probably Czech than German,
and although the composer was born on German soil he was
sent at an early age to Bohemia for his musical education.
From Prague he went to Milan, thanks to a generous patron,
and he began his career as a composer of Italian operas in the
conventional style described in the previous chapter. By the
end of his life he had composed 107 operas, including ballets

and dramatic cantatas; and 92 of these were first produced in Italian cities. Eight more came out at the Italian opera in London. Not one of his operas was written to German words; those which he wrote for the court of Vienna were either in Italian or French – the French operas being little comic operas for a French troupe engaged to entertain the court at Schönbrunn. Gluck told Dr Burney, who called on him at Vienna in 1770, that the turning point of his career was his visit to London in 1746. The two operas which he produced in London that year were complete failures; but if his statement to Burney was anything more than a piece of politeness to an English critic, it meant that he had heard the music of Handel (1746 was the year of *Judas Maccabaeus*). And there is no doubt that he was deeply influenced by the operas of Rameau, which he saw in Paris.

In 1761 Gluck made the acquaintance of an Italian poet, Raniero de' Calzabigi, who had come to live at Vienna. Calzabigi had spent some time in Paris, and was interested in the aesthetic problem of musical drama. He had also read a book about opera written in 1756 by another cosmopolitan Italian, Count Algarotti, who had been nine years at the court of Frederick the Great in Berlin. The result of Calzabigi's collaboration with Gluck was the famous opera *Orfeo*, first produced in Italian at Vienna in 1762. *Orfeo* is a landmark in the history of opera, and it is the one opera by Gluck which is fairly well known at the present day. Modern audiences think of it as a work which takes them far away from the melodramatic world of Verdi or the luscious eroticism of Wagner and Richard Strauss into a region of unearthly dignity and classicality, a world inhabited not by men and women but by marble statues miraculously endowed with life and motion. To Gluck's first audience it must have been a curious experiment which defied all the current traditions. Calzabigi set out to create something like an opera by Rameau in Italian. The general scheme of the opera is French, with its innumerable choruses and ballets; there was nothing new about the visions of Hades and the Elysian Fields – Rameau had pictured these regions long before. But the words were Italian, and that meant that the music was largely Italian in character, although both librettist and composer were determined to make no concessions to the Italian taste for florid singing. It was a complete break with the conventions on both sides, except for the overture, which is rather paltry, and the final chorus, which has all the prettiness of Rameau's ballets of graces and loves, shepherdesses and female sailors; otherwise all that world of Watteau and Fragonnard is severely disdained. Both words and music are intensely concentrated on the story of Orpheus and Eurydice, and on every shade of feeling experienced by hero and heroine in the course of the drama. Modern audiences perhaps hardly realize this. *Orfeo* is not very often performed nowadays and when it is given, attention is always drawn to the fact that the part of Orpheus is one for a great contralto, with the result that far too much fuss is made about the way in which the lady sings the famous (and curiously inappropriate) air, 'Che farô senza Euridice?' If the opera is sung in a foreign language the sense of the recitatives is missed, and most people come away with the impression that the best things in the opera are the ballets.

The oddity of this opera can only be realized by those who have some acquaintance with the other operas of the period. Everything points to its having been an experimental work addressed to a limited public of intellectuals; it must be remembered that the court of Maria Theresa was unusually musical, and that members of the imperial family often took part in musical performances themselves. *Orfeo* has only three characters, Orpheus, Eurydice and Cupid, instead of the usual six or seven; it has no tenor or bass parts except in the chorus. In spite of its French construction it is in three acts like an Italian opera, instead of five, like a French one; it has few changes of scene compared with other operas of the period, and it is also a good deal shorter. And the whole libretto has much more affinity with the Italian operas on the same subject by Peri and Monteverdi than with either Metastasio or the authors of Rameau's French librettos. In all probability the subject of Orpheus was deliberately chosen as being symbolical of this reversion, for the musical and dramatic theories put forward by Calzabigi and Algarotti, afterwards to be claimed by Wagner as his own, were nothing more than those which had been proclaimed by the first creators of opera round about 1600.

Orfeo was followed by *Alceste* (1767) and *Paride ed Elena* (1770), both to words by Calazabigi. *Paris and Helen* is never performed now, but it is a work of extraordinary beauty. Like *Orfeo,* it has only three characters, Paris, Helen and Cupid, and the whole opera is taken up with the inner development of their emotions. There is a great deal of elaborate ballet, by way of interlude and decoration, but even less action takes place on the stage than in Wagner's *Tristan and Isolde,* to which Gluck's opera bears certain resemblance. But it would be a difficult opera to put on the stage, because of the huge burden thrown on the two chief characters.

For the moment these experimental operas of Gluck made very little mark, and he had to go on composing others in the old-fashioned Metastasian form. Metastasio himself had been living in Vienna since 1729, and he died there in 1782. But in 1772 Du Roullet, an attaché at the French Embassy, arranged Racine's play *Iphigénie en Aulide* for Gluck, and two years later, with the help of his pupil Marie Antoinette, who was married to the Dauphin, Gluck was invited to produce this new opera in Paris. *Iphigénie en Aulide* was followed by French versions of *Orfeo* and *Alceste* but although the success of these operas was beyond question, an opposition party brought forward the Neapolitan composer Piccinni as a rival. As had happened twenty years earlier in the case of the *bouffons,* a war of journalists was started over Gluck and Piccinni. Piccinni had made a considerable name for himself as a composer of comic operas, and the heroine of one of them, *La Buona Figliuola* (Rome, 1760), has given her name to a railway station just outside Rome Cecchina.* He was an extremely modest man, and had not the slightest wish to be dragged into a quarrel with Gluck, for whom he had a great admiration. A further embarrassment to him was the fact that he knew hardly a word of French. But the journalists who wanted to damage Gluck insisted on his composing an *Iphigénie en Tauride* as a rival to Gluck's setting of that subject in the same year and the result for poor Piccinni was disastrous. This was in 1779; in 1780 Gluck went back to Vienna.

* Other operatic railway stations are Swiss Cottage (London) after Adolphe Adam's *Le Châlet* (called in England *The Swiss Cottage* and Szép Ilona (Budapest), named after *La Belle Hélène* (Offenbach).

In 1784 he was commissioned to write another opera for Paris on a libretto by Calzabigi, *Les Danaïdes*, but as he was too ill to undertake it, the music was written by his pupil Salieri and performed under their joint names. After the twelfth performance, when the opera was an assured success, Gluck let it be known that the whole opera was the work of Salieri.

The most satisfactory opera of Gluck is *Armide* (Paris, 1777), on a libretto of Quinault that had once been set by Lully; the same story was made into an opera by Handel — *Rinaldo* (London, 1711). Gluck was never a technically accomplished composer, and his untidiness of style makes his operas curiously difficult to sing, conduct or produce, in spite of moments which achieve overwhelming dramatic effects. The literary formality of *Armide* gives it unity, and as it belongs to the last period of Gluck's career it is less experimental and more assured in technique than any of the others. To stage it is, however, a considerable undertaking, for it makes great demands on the singers, and in addition requires elaborate ballets and scenic effects. The two *Iphigénies* used to be performed fairly often in Germany, but have been revived in England (within recent years) only for isolated productions, generally by amateurs.

At the present moment, when all operatic enterprise, even in countries where opera is heavily subsidized by the government, is precarious, and all managers have to concentrate their energies on popular successes, the chance of seeing an opera by Gluck is small, whether we hope for a sumptuous production in Paris or Berlin, or a modest one at Falmouth or Toynbee Hall. But in each case it is safe to say that a Gluck opera, whichever one it may be, is always a remarkable experience, at any rate to those who enter a theatre to enjoy opera as a work of art rather than to pose as connoisseurs of singing or conducting. After nearly two centuries we can admit that Gluck achieved his object of making everything subservient to the drama, and not even in *Orfeo* has a star singer much of an opportunity. The star conductor is even worse off.

Gluck has gone down to posterity as the great reformer of the opera, thanks mainly to the writings of Wagner, who was glad to claim and utilize him as a primitive forerunner of his own gospel. But it must not be supposed that Gluck's successes in Paris led to performances all over the operatic world, such as followed some of the well-known operas of the nineteenth century – *Les Huguenots, Faust, Carmen* or *Cavalleria Rusticana*. In the eighteenth century an opera which had been successful in one city might be performed in several others, but even then it did not get taken up into a permanent standard repertory and repeated year after year as has been the case with *Cavalleria Rusticana* ever since 1890. The eighteenth century had no 'reverence for the classics'; that doctrine was probably started by the Handel-worshippers in England, and in any case it was never applied to Handel's operas. In operatic circles people wanted new operas, just as they want new plays at the present day. The building up of a standard repertory in opera could only begin when there were a very large number of opera houses open every night for long seasons. And there were other causes which must have hindered it – the perpetual production of novelties and the growing commercialization of opera, especially in Italy. The catalogue of opera librettos in the Library of Congress at Washington, which does not go beyond 1800, includes some 25,000 titles, most of which are Italian. Out of those 25,000 how many are familiar to any modern conductor, singer, publisher, critic, or amateur? One in a thousand would be a liberal estimate. In the half-century 1800–1850 the rate of production must have been far greater, but the number of survivors is small compared to the number of immediate successes, and the number of successes must have been far eclipsed by that of the failures. Every composer hoped to make his fortune out of an opera in those days, and the obvious way to achieve success was to imitate success already achieved. And when hundreds of operas were all much the same thing and no more, it was only natural that few were handed on to posterity. How the choice came to be made is often very mysterious.

Gluck's operas were certainly imitated by some of his immediate followers, but not for very long, and never with any very great success. Salieri, his favourite pupil, is now remembered mainly as the man who was alleged to have poisoned Mozart; his numerous operas, which if not as good as

Mozart's are at least better than most of their contemporaries', are almost all in the Italian comic style. Mozart's *Idomeneo* (1781), composed when he was twenty-four, might have served as a lesson to Gluck to show him how his own operas ought to have been written; but *Idomeneo* has had far fewer subsequent performances than any of Gluck's famous operas, and from Mozart's point of view it was old-fashioned at the time it was conceived. The rest of Mozart's operatic output, although it certainly contains occasional reminiscences of Gluck, is in an entirely different tradition. What was important in Gluck's operas, as in Gluck's own mind, was not the technical method but the moral outlook, and in so far as Gluck had any style of his own, that style could only be imitated by someone with the same philosophical principles. The musical style of Gluck's ballets and marches, like his well-known 'high-priest' manner, was to a larger extent common property. When Mozart appropriated these things he executed them a great deal better. Gluck could never be imitated commercially; he could not even serve as a model from which to learn construction or any technical methods. He could only be venerated as the expression of a moral ideal; and for that he still stands even now.

The chief operatic centres of Europe had by this time shifted to Paris and Vienna. Vienna was almost an Italian city, as far as music was concerned; the symphonic school which made Vienna famous in the days of Haydn and Mozart was the joint product of Italian vocal music and the Slav talent for instrumental virtuosity. And Vienna always kept in touch with Paris for all aspects of cultural life. Besides that, Vienna was a junction for the northern capitals; from Vienna the comic operas of Venice were handed on to Prague, Berlin, Copenhagen, Stockholm, Warsaw and St Petersburg. The imperial court still demanded serious Italian opera for state occasions, but as the century drew to its end it became clear that Metastasian opera was a thing of the past, and comic opera, Italian or French, the only thing that people really wanted to see.

The French called their own comic operas by the title of *Comédie mêlée d'ariettes*, comedy mixed with little songs, and right up to the very end of the century there were many of these in which the spoken comedy is so complete in itself that the songs might easily be omitted. Beaumarchais' play *Le Barbier de Séville* was originally written as a comic opera of this kind. It might generally be said that in France the play was better than the music, and the music in Italy better than the play. Italian comic opera was very much a matter of routine; in France there was far more variety of subject, and towards the end of the century Italian composers began to take librettos that had already had a success in Paris and get them translated into Italian for their own use. It is often interesting to compare the French and Italian versions of the same opera.

Very much in the background, there was a native German opera, but it had always been a humble affair, and it was not until about 1820 that German opera began to establish itself on a sure foundation. The first German opera was the *Daphne* of Heinrich Schütz (Torgau, 1627); the libretto was a translation of Rinuccini's Florentine opera. All trace of the music is lost, and we have little information about later German attempts at opera; they were almost always on religious subjects. Hamburg established a permanent German opera house in 1678; here, too, religious subjects were preferred at first, for the local clergy fancied themselves as poets and at the same time followed the example of Jeremy Collier in denouncing the wickedness of the stage. Life in Hamburg at that time must have been very like that of Restoration London, only a good deal coarser and more violent. The most successful composer at Hamburg was Reinhard Keiser (1673–1739); his first opera anticipated *The Beggar's Opera* in dealing with the career of a local highwayman recently executed. But as Hamburg society became more cultivated it demanded Italian opera, and Keiser produced several works in which the songs are in Italian and the recitatives in German. Handel's German opera *Almira* (1704) was written for Hamburg, but in 1706 he went to Italy, and that was the end of his career as a German composer. Some of his London operas were, however, performed at Hamburg in German, and other German operas were composed by his former friend Mattheson.

Much more popular were the trivial comic operas of Johann Adam Hiller (1728–1804), which like the French *vaudevilles* were comedies with incidental songs. The simplest way of obtaining a general idea of what comic opera was like in Germany in the days of Mozart and Beethoven is to look through Beethoven's collected sets of variations for the pianoforte, for several sets are on tunes from these pieces, and obviously they must have been the most popular ones. The French and Italian airs are pretty thin stuff, but they sound classical by the side of the German tunes, which are paltry in the extreme. No wonder Mozart in adolescence was furious at the idea of composing a German opera!

The operas which Mozart wrote before *Idomeneo*, beginning with one composed at the age of eight, have a certain interest as biographical documents, but they are of no importance in the general history of opera. His next work after *Idomeneo* was a German comic opera, *Die Entführung aus dem Serail* (*The Abduction from the Seraglio*), written in 1782 by command of the Emperor Joseph II, who had conceived the idea of establishing a national German opera. *The Seraglio* is seldom performed, for it requires exceptional singers. Each number, taken by itself, is a masterpiece of style and characterization; but regarded as a whole, the opera is a bewildering jumble; one of the most important characters, the Pasha, never sings at all, so that he remains completely outside the musical scheme, and after a number of songs and ensembles on the grand scale the opera ends with a conventional little French finale in which each character sings a verse and the rest join in a refrain. *The Seraglio* had a certain influence on Weber's *Oberon* more than forty years later, but it cannot be said to have founded a school, and although it was a success when first produced, the German opera house was a failure.

Mozart's next three operas, *The Marriage of Figaro* (1787), *Don Giovanni* (1788), and *Così fan Tutte* (*The School for Lovers*) (1790), are all Italian comic operas to words by Mozart's happiest collaborator, the Abbé Lorenzo da Ponte. In the field of Italian comic opera neither Mozart nor Da Ponte stood alone and undisputed. Da Ponte had a hated rival in the Abbé G. B. Casti; Casti had a most venomous tongue, and it is a pity that he never got his librettos set to music by Mozart, for they are extremely amusing. Unfortunately he was associated with Paisiello and Salieri, who were far beneath Mozart in genius, though at that time much more popular with the public. At the present day Mozart is regarded as the one supremely perfect artist in the history of music; in his own day the same accusation was brought against him as was brought against Handel, Wagner and various later composers of opera – that they did not know how to write for the voice and that they made far too much noise with the orchestra.

This question of orchestral noise in opera is a very interesting one, but it shall be reserved for a later chapter dealing with all sorts of musical technicalities. Here it suffices to say that what really annoyed Mozart's listeners was the fact that he took much more trouble over the orchestra than his rivals did. A barren and empty score can often sound much more unpleasantly noisy than one which is full of ingenious and expressive details; but Mozart's audiences did not want to be bothered with the mental exertion of following such things. 'Too many notes, my dear Mozart!' was the Emperor's criticism. Napoleon preferred Paisiello's flimsy sentimentalities to the more solid works of Cherubini, and William II had no use for the composer of *Salome* and *Elektra*.

Mozart's operas have suffered the sad fate of becoming classics. After he was dead people began to make him into a romantic. *The Marriage of Figaro* was almost a revolutionary manifesto; later generations, especially in places where the opera was patronized by a court and aristocracy, interpreted it as a piece of Dresden china prettiness. *Don Giovanni* was romanticized first into a tragedy and in our own day treated as a study in sexual pathology. *Così fan Tutte* was treated seriously and found so shocking that it had to be provided with a variety of new librettos, none of which ever brought it success.

To turn Beaumarchais' comedy *Le Mariage de Figaro* into an Italian comic opera was a very bold undertaking. The original play to which it was the sequel, *Le Barbier de Séville*, had indeed been planned as a French comic opera modelled on old-fashioned Italian lines. Beaumarchais took what was then a worn-out convention of Italian opera, and in his own personal and original way turned it into a new sort of comedy.

The result is that *The Barber* made an admirable libretto for Paisiello and Rossini, both of them composers who preferred conventions to novelties. But in the second play little trace of old Italian comedy is left and the author's main intention is social and political satire. It may be conceded that satire of this kind cannot be expressed in music; but all the same it is certain that both Mozart and Da Ponte were men who would appreciate this type of satire to the full. The original play had been forbidden for some years in Paris; it had been released in 1784, and had become the talk of intellectual Europe. In 1786 the play was still forbidden in Vienna, where authority was more nervous than in French. It was the play that everybody was talking about and that everybody wanted to see; and surely an English reader of today can understand how a piece that was forbidden as a play in the language of the people could none the less be put on the stage as an Italian opera. From a hack librettist's point of view it was no easy task to make the transformation. The play was in five acts; comic operas were generally in three, sometimes even in two. All sorts of purely musical conventions had to be considered, such as the building up of complicated finales that brought an act to an end with all the characters on the stage in a row, shouting at the top of their voices. Da Ponte and Mozart managed it, though the opera had to be in four acts, and long ones at that. The modern spectator who enjoys *The Marriage of Figaro* today has no idea of the trouble and worry that the making of that opera must have caused to Da Ponte and Mozart, and the further trouble and worry that it must have caused to all concerned in the first performance because it did not conform to the standard routine. Only the determination to get political satire past a watchful censor could have stimulated so much perserverance and tenacity. Conventional-minded people who like to think that admiration of Mozart is always in good taste often say that he was wise to leave out all the satirical element in Beaumarchais. Mozart's audience probably knew quite well what was missing, even if the singers (as often happens on the operatic stage) knew only their own individual parts and had no intimate understanding of those. And if anyone in Vienna saw the significance of this play, which deals with the way in which a gentleman of pleasure treats his domestic servants, it should have been Mozart himself, who had been nothing better than a domestic servant in the days when he was employed by the Archbishop of Salzburg. At Salzburg he must have had personal acquaintance enough with Figaro, Susanna, and the Reverend Don Basilio, too.

A careful study of *Don Giovanni* shows clearly that what was in the mind of Da Ponte and Mozart was to repeat the success of *Figaro*. Here again Da Ponte adapted an older play; but this time, instead of having a carefully finished comedy to translate, he had only an older Italian libretto to re-write, the last of a long line of adaptations going back for two hundred years. It was a clumsy piece of work, and the author had himself made an apology for it in the shape of a prologue representing that favourite subject of comic opera composers in the eighteenth century, a theatrical company in difficulties. Everyone is in comic despair. What are they to perform, as a last chance of saving themselves from ruin? Someone suggests *The Stone Guest*, and it is evident that if the company had been English, that character might have suggested *Punch and Judy*, from the way in which the idea is received. The old story of *Don Giovanni* (Shadwell had put it on the English stage with music by Purcell) was the puppet-play known to everybody, laughed at by everybody, and yet eternally new. It was the obvious subject to repeat the success of *Figaro*; it was the story of the gentleman of pleasure and his comic manservant. That comic servant, who appears in hundreds of operas, is Harlequin, here and in *Figaro* – the knave who looks like a fool, the mouthpiece through which the poet claims his right to criticize the world, the link between the stage and the audience. In the French theatre, the painted drapery just inside the proscenium is still called the *manteau d'Arlequin*, because it was where Harlequin popped in and out to talk confidentially to the audience.

Why so many people, especially those of an older generation, should insist on taking *Don Giovanni* as a serious opera is a curious problem of musical psychology and aesthetics. In the Byronic age people wanted *all* music to be romantic; later on Mozart became a classic, and every great singer, male or female, had to pass the test of being heard in the appropriate Mozartian part. *Don Giovanni,* composed for a tiny theatre, was transferred to the enormous stages of Berlin, Paris and London. Intimacy of interpretation became impossible, and gradually the opera became so famous that only singers of established reputation, and of corresponding age and bulk, were expected to appear in it. By that time the story of the opera had become a thing to which nobody gave a moment's thought; one went to see Lablache as Leporello, or Patti as Zerlina. The character of *Don Giovanni* himself fascinated men of letters – and it must be remembered that *Don Giovanni* was not the sole property of Mozart – so that all sorts of attempts were made to explain his amorous propensities and turn him into a sort of Nietzschean superman, in order to evade the difficulty of reconciling his conduct with the ordinary behaviour of a gentleman.

The simplest plan is to take the opera as its author and composer intended – as an amusing comedy, with a touch of social satire and a great deal of fantastic impossibility. If *Don Giovanni* were to be acted in plain prose as a straight, serious play without music it would be intolerably revolting. It is bearable only in the spirit of a puppet play, where nothing is real and morality has no concern. And those who are obsessed by Don Giovanni's irresistible sex-appeal may be reminded that in Mozart's opera every one of his love affairs lands him in a humiliating and ridiculous situation.

Così fan Tutte (The School for Lovers) is an elaborate artificial comedy, but as opera singers are seldom expert in that style of acting it is only too often played as a knockabout farce, for which Mozart's exquisite music is indeed inappropriate. It has never enjoyed the success of the other two famous operas of Mozart, and the blame has always been laid on the libretto. Mozart has never enjoyed much success in Italy at any time, so that the neglect of this work in that country is understandable. It was occasionally performed in Italian in London, but English audiences must have found the words difficult to follow. In Germany it was, of course, given in German; the recitatives were spoken, and the translation was clumsy. German musicians and critics made up their minds firmly that the story was impossible (which it may be, though that has not been an invariable cause of operatic failure), and also that it was repulsive, because two very silly young women are gently taught a useful lesson by a cynical old bachelor. The compatriots of Schumann and Wagner have never wished to make fun of sentimentality, especially when associated with classical music; woman was an ideal that ought never to be made ridiculous. Young English people of today would more probably say that Mozart's two romantic heroes are charmingly absurd, and the two heroines delightfully Victorian; in fact, the recent productions of *Così fan Tutte* in English at Sadler's Wells have been the first since Mozart's day, in any country, to achieve really popular success.

In the last year of his life (1791) Mozart composed two operas. One was *La Clemenza di Tito*, a ceremonial affair in the old formal Italian tradition. The other was *The Magic Flute*, written for a popular theatre on the outskirts of Vienna; it started to be a spectacular fairy play and ended as an allegory of Freemasonry. Early in the eighteenth century Freemasonry had spread to Germany from England, and it made rapid progress, especially among intellectuals, because it stood for what we should now call liberal humanitarianism. Mozart had been initiated in 1785, and Schikaneder, the manager of the theatre, was also a devoted Freemason. But Freemasonry has always been condemned by the Catholic Church, and it was severely repressed by Maria Theresa, although her own husband, the Emperor Francis I, was himself a member of the craft.

The Magic Flute is Mozart's greatest work for the stage, and is the foundation of all subsequent German opera. Although it set out to be nothing more than a comic play with songs, and a large part for Schikaneder himself (Papageno) in which he could put in plenty of gags and talk to the audience in the old Harlequin style, it developed into something like a morality play of the deepest ethical significance, but remote from any suggestion of orthodox religion. It is perhaps the one work of Mozart in which he achieved real sublimity.

CHAPTER FOUR

OPERA UNDER THE FRENCH REVOLUTION –
THE BEGINNINGS OF ROMANTIC OPERA –
BEETHOVEN – ROSSINI – WEBER

It is generally supposed that the history of French comic opera is of interest only to Frenchmen, and to few even of them. To English opera-goers the names of Mosigny, Philidor, Grétry and Dalayrac are almost unknown. A few songs from these old operas have been printed in anthologies and are occasionally sung at concerts – probably the best-known specimen is 'Plaisir d'amour', by a German called Schwartzendorf, who assumed the Italian name of Martini and composed comic operas in French. Paris then, as always, was full of foreign musicans, mainly Italian and German at that time. Italians were only too glad to emigrate, and Germans thought they had more chance of making their fortunes in Paris and London than at home, where Italians secured all the best jobs. French audiences seem to have cared more about good acting than about good singing. If one compares, as one sometimes can, the French and Italian settings of the same book and almost the same words, one sees that the Italians made a far more brilliant show-piece for the singer, but that the French aimed chiefly at the natural expression of words.

The French plots show far more variety and interest than the Italian. We find plenty of what we may call 'village opera', but Grétry and Dalayrac went much further afield, experimenting in medieval chivalry, Eastern romance, fairyland, England, sentimentality after Richardson and horrors after Mrs Radcliffe. As far as literary material was concerned, the romantic movement was well under way in French comic opera before the Revolution, but the romantic style of music was yet to be developed. The outbreak of the Revolution gave a startling impulse to French opera. New theatres were opened, and new composers started writing for a new sort of public. The change of style is so gradual that it is difficult to analyse and describe, but generally speaking both the plays and the music written for them became more intense and vehement. Sentimental comedy developed into romantic drama or into what we should now call melodrama; and melodrama was in fact invented by French authors just at the end of the century. It was called melodrama because music played a large part in it, and sometimes it is difficult to decide whether a work is to be considered as a play with music or as an opera with spoken dialogue. The chief characteristic of the music in these French Revolution operas is the extension of the single musical numbers and especially of those for several characters. We see at this period the beginning of a desire to carry on the action within the course of a musical number, instead of leaving that duty to plain recitative or spoken words. But simultaneously there is a musical development which is purely technical, the tendency to treat these ensembles as if they were instrumental symphonies, with a great deal of formal repetition of phrases and a huge piling up of voices and instruments towards the end. It is in this period that we notice more and more the establishment of all those operatic conventions which have made opera ludicrous in the eyes of the plain man.

The various governments of the Revolution were all agreed in recognizing the educative influence of the theatre, and the opera reflected this doctrine in a number of dramas based on stories of ancient Rome. But the general public probably preferred the dramas of more or less contemporary life, and the spectacular operas that ended with a shipwreck or a burning castle, the hero throwing himself from the top of a rock into the sea, or traversing a rickety bridge to rescue the heroine and bring her in a state of collapse to the front of the stage. Cherubini was the most accomplished composer of spectacular operas; his *Lodoiska* (1791) ends with a conflagration and his *Elise* (1794) with an avalanche in the Alps – it is an early operatic example of the romantic interest in Switzerland. Lesueur's *La Caverne* is a story of a fair lady captured by brigands in Italy; at the end the brigand chief turns out to be her long-lost brother who has left his aristocratic home and gone to the bad. The same composer won the admiration of Napoleon for an opera called *Ossian ou Les Bardes*, one of the many operas in which the musical representation of a storm is a conspicuous feature. The French romantic period is full of operatic storms.

The French also created what is sometimes called the 'rescue opera' – a type of libretto in which the hero or heroine is shut up in prison by a villainous tyrant; the wife or husband attempts to set the prisoner free, but generally makes the situation far worse, and the invariable happy end is brought about by the sudden entry of a chorus of soldiers who arrest the tyrant. This useful scheme was first exhibited in an opera by Berton, *Les Rigueurs du Cloître* (1790), the object of which was to cast odium on the religious life. The scene is laid in a convent, where a young nun who has been caught receiving a love-letter is tried by the abbess and senior nuns and condemned to be imprisoned in the cellar. Just as she is being pushed down the steps a detachment of the National Guard burst in, headed by her own young man as the officer in command; he informs the nuns that monastic vows are declared invalid and that it is the duty of every woman sufficiently young to get married and produce a family. The music of this opera is not very interesting, but the libretto has a great deal of humour.

Most of these French comic operas were translated into German and formed the staple repertory of the German theatres. The situation in Germany from about 1800 to 1830 was very much like that of our own country a hundred years later. The courts and the fashionable society surrounding them patronized Italian opera while native opera had to struggle along as best it could. There was often a considerable demand for popular opera in the language of the people, but most of it was French or Italian in origin. German opera of that period must not be judged by the standard of Mozart, Beethoven and Weber. We know from the life of Weber how difficult it was to get Mozart's operas performed and appreciated at Prague and Dresden; Beethoven's one opera was never a success, and Weber's own unhappy career was a perpetual struggle against Italian intrigue. Even German historians say as little as possible about the minor German opera composers of those days. The records of various German theatres are accessible, and it has been shown that Beethoven, during the time that he lived at Bonn, must have heard (and played in) hardly anything but French and Italian opera; at Vienna the various theatres giving opera from 1800 onwards kept up the same repertory. Grétry, Dalayrac, Méhul, Catel, Cherubini, with the Italians Paisiello, Paer, Mayr (a completely Italianized German who spent most of his life at Bergamo) – and later on Rossini: the Germans had no chance against them, and German opera in Vienna meant the trivialities of Weigl and Wranitzky.

Beethoven's *Fidelio* (first version 1805, second 1806, third 1814) was based on the libretto of a typical French 'rescue-opera' which had been set to music by Gaveaux in 1798. The author, J. N. Bouilly, vouched for its being a true story of the Reign of Terror, though he transplanted it to Spain in the sixteenth century for fear of the characters being identified. This first French version was less of an opera and more of a play with music than Beethoven's. The next stage of the work is an Italian adaptation set to music by Paer at Dresden in 1804; Paer's music is very serious and sincere, but it still preserves the general outline of the French popular opera. Beethoven started his work in just the same spirit but gradually (especially after later revisions) developed it into something more like a dramatic symphony. The music becomes too great for the play, and as modern audiences hear it with the experience of all or many of Beethoven's symphonies and other great concert works, they are often disappointed with the opera as a whole.

Beethoven's personality was profoundly affected by the social and political upheavals of his time. We are often told that his music was the natural development of the music of Haydn and Mozart, and historians have pointed out the direct resemblances to these two predecessors. But nobody can fail to recognize that even in Beethoven's first period there is a new musical character which cannot be derived from Haydn and Mozart, and it is no belittling of Beethoven's genius to admit that this came to him from the music of the French Revolution. Modern critics often find the characters in *Fidelio* impossibly unreal; Florestan, the imprisoned hero, is too virtuous, and Pizarro, the typical 'tyrant', too incredibly villainous.

They forget that this exaggeration is the inevitable consequence of the musical form, and that the musical form is that of its period. Compared with most operas in the repertory, *Fidelio* is unusually short, but the single musical numbers all appear to be very long, because most of the action belongs to the spoken dialogue. Here we strike what was the main obstacle to the progress of German opera – the incompetence of the German librettists. They must have know perfectly well that the musical technique of Beethoven's day insisted on perpetual repetitions of phrase; but they never seemed to ask themselves whether their words would bear repetition or not. Repetition was nothing new; Handel repeats words, but the Italian poets of his day, and the English ones, too, when they wrote for music, chose words which were not rendered ridiculous by repetition.

It must be admitted that Beethoven's invariable preoccupation with moral ideas leads him to emphasize and repeat single words, such as *Freiheit* (freedom), which stirred his deepest emotions, as they did those of Byron and Shelley; the result is that throughout the opera Beethoven is constantly forgetting the drama to contemplate something beyond it. His characers have no time to show themselves as anything more than 'hero', 'heroine' or 'villain', and there is no need why they should. In a modern play we should discover their characters from their actions; they would not talk about their inward feelings in solioquy. But it is only since the days of Ibsen that soliloquy has gone out of fashion on the stage; and we accept the frequent soliloquies of Mozart without criticism. The reason why the same thing is resented in *Fidelio* is probably that whereas Mozart seems to confront us with an utterly unreal world, Beethoven is still near enough to our own time to make us feel that Florestan and Leonora are real people, so real at certain moments that their purely musical formalities (which in Beethoven's symphonies we take for granted) can hardly help causing us discomfort.

Florestan and Leonora were indeed real people once. Beethoven has made them eternal types; they are Mozart's Tamino and Pamina come to earth. German stage-directors after the revolution of 1918 saw them as man and woman of their own time; they are alive for us today, and Pizarro too.

The Napoleonic period is well represented in opera by Spontini, whose most famous opera, *La Vestale* (Paris, 1807), is not yet quite forgotten, although it must be a great many years since it was performed in England. It was given a very sumptuous production at Florence in 1933, and it was said at the time that it had been chosen because it symbolized the sacrifice of the individual to the state. Spontini's next opera, *Fernand Cortez* (1808), is mentioned by historians as the beginning of the 'noisy' school of operas; it is also a landmark in many other respects. It is the first of the 'historico-political' operas of the nineteenth century illustrating episodes from modern history with everything on a colossal scale, requiring a huge theatre with complicated realistic scenery, innumerable chorus singers, dancers and supers, military bands on the stage and principals with immensely powerful voices.

By this time Paris had become practically the only centre of operatic activity. Vienna ceased to be of any importance; operas were always being performed there, but Vienna neither created operas nor attracted foreign composers to create them, as Paris did. Italy was always productive, but Paris was the goal of every Italian ambition. The Italian school had divided into two groups, the perpetuators of the old tradition according to which the opera ought to consist almost entirely of solo songs, and the innovators who wished to adopt French principles, adapting French librettos, with more ensemble music and less recitative. There emerges at this time a type of opera called *opera semi-seria*, although the title is never very consistently employed; it was something between serious opera and comic, leaning heavily towards the sentimental and even towards the romantic. French influence encouraged more use of chorus and ballet; and it must be remembered that chorus and ballet had originally been one and the same thing, as in ancient Greece. The chorus seem to have been the dancers in the early Italian operas, and although in Rameau's operas they were separate bodies, they were very often on the stage together, utilizing the same music; the chorus sang it and the dancers danced to it, sometimes to the singing, sometimes to an instrumental version, hence in later operas the chorus is often introduced more like a ballet than like characters taking part in the drama; the reader will probably remember English operas and operettas which begin with an 'opening chorus' who inform the audience that 'we are' gipsies, soldiers, fairies, or anything else convenient.

All this means a gradual break-up of the 'class distinctions' of earlier opera. A larger public for opera was growing up; pit and gallery began to count for more than the boxes did in determining success or failure. The first half of the nineteenth century shows a ruthless commercialization of opera, and no people had a sharper eye for 'realities' than the Italians. Opera became what it is still, an important item in the Italian export trade.

The two most successful business men of the operatic world were Domenico Barbaja (1778–1841), who began his career as a waiter, continued as a circus manager, and finally became director of two opera houses in Vienna, the San Carlo Theatre at Naples and the Scala at Milan all at the same time; and Gioacchino Rossini (1792–1868), called by Italian historians the 'Napoleon of Music'. Rossini is remembered now only by two operas, *The Barber of Seville* (Rome, 1816) and *William Tell* (Paris, 1829); of the others, which indeed conquered all Europe, the modern world knows no more than a few overtures and selections for military band. The opera which first made him famous was *Tancredi* (1813).

All the Italian operas of this period depended for their success on the singers. This was nothing new, for the same thing could have been said of opera in the days of Handel. The school of which Rossini is the head achieved their popularity not merely by the florid and showy music which they composed for all the voices, for tenors and basses as well as for sopranos and contraltos, but very largely by the adoption into serious opera of methods hitherto restricted to musical comedy. What the general public has always wanted was to hear the greatest singers in the most trivial music. Rossini had among his many gifts a genius for triviality. The Napoleonic wars had given a great impetus to military music of all kinds; one can note that influence constantly even in Beethoven himself. Schubert wrote large quantities of military music which is still the delight of pianoforte duet-players, and the minor composers of Vienna exploited the military atmosphere wherever they could. It runs all through Rossini's operas, though Rossini had not invented it himself; most of the mannerisms which we generally associate with Rossini are to be found in Paer as early as 1800, at any rate in the germ. It was this irresistible rhythmic energy that marched Rossini's operas across Europe. To hear the overture to *William Tell* is always an exciting experience; to strum through half a dozen of Rossini's forgotten operas is wearisome and monotonous.

Lord Mount Edgcumbe (1764–1839), whose *Reminiscences of the Opera* (1825) is a valuable and interesting document for the history of musical taste in those days, found Rossini's music noisy and vulgar. He hated Rossini's battering ensembles and finales, and the perpetual crash of his trombones; well he might, for this aggressive noisiness was the vice of all the Italians in those days. It was the Italians of a hundred years earlier who had invented what one might call the orchestral *claque*. In the days of Bach and Handel court etiquette forbade applause unless the prince himself chose to lead it; consequently their musical movements finish without the re-iterated chords of dominant and tonic that mark the end of all symphonies and concertos in the days of Mozart. That, needless to say, was started by the Italians, not to cover up the noise of applause – what Italian ever disliked noise? – but to stir up the audience to begin clapping and shouting. Rossini had a great sense of humour as well as a keen eye to business, and *The Barber* consciously and purposely exaggerates these devices, partly to make fun of them and also to make the most of them. But it is a sign, as old Lord Mount Edgcumbe saw, that the days of aristocratic opera were over.

To the same epoch belong Donizetti and Bellini, still national heroes in Italy, if hardly even names to the present day frequenters of Sadler's Wells. Donizetti's *Lucia di Lammermoor* (Naples, 1835) was one of the many operas based on the novels and poems of Sir Walter Scott; it is a *prima donna*'s opera, culminating in the heroine's 'mad scene'. Scott, Shakespeare and Schiller had just been discovered by the Continent; but the numerous operatic heroines who go mad generally remind us more of Tilburina than of Ophelia. It was in these days that the manager-husband of a great *prima donna* said that the only requirements for an opera season were '*ma femme et cinq poupés*' – his own wife and five puppets.

It is about this time, too, that the 'happy end' ceases to be obligatory; in fact, from Donizetti (1797–1848) onwards the majority of Italian operas and many of other countries end in tragedy. The most obvious source of this tendency was no doubt Victor Hugo, whose romantic dramas began to appear in 1829; several of them were seized on by composers as foundations for librettos. But the unhappy end may be traced much farther back, if we adopt a truly romantic point of view and regard the villain as the hero; Don Giovanni at once poses the question for a generation brought up on Byronic Satanism. And it is just at this time that Italian comic opera suddenly disappears altogether from the stage, though Donizetti had written three which are among the best examples of the type – *The Daughter of the Regiment* (1840), *Don Pasquale* (Paris, 1834) and *L'Elisir d'Amore* (1832). Rossini's *Barber of Seville* still holds the stage everywhere as the only comic opera which can approach those of Mozart.

Bellini (1801–35) stands in a rather different category; noise and vulgarity were foreign to his temperament, and his music shows a delicacy and refinement that were indeed rare in the Italian theatre of his time. He never had the slick professionalism of Rossini, and his workmanship was often very amateurish, though his charm of melody was both individual and attractive. Two of his operas are still remembered, at any rate in Italy. *La Sonnambula* (Milan, 1831) is an *opera semiseria* about a village maiden in Switzerland who walks in her sleep with results disastrous to her reputation; after some misunderstandings her innocence is established and all ends happily. Bellini was fortunate in having an accomplished man of letters as his librettist, Felice Romani, who understood how to express every shade of sentiment in language that was simple and unaffected; it is probable, too, that Bellini had some knowledge of the French composers, for he stands apart from the other Italians of his time in the natural, almost conversational, way in which he handles words.

More famous was *Norma* (Milan, 1831) a tragic story of a Druidess in ancient Gaul during the occupation by the Romans. Like Spontini's Vestal virgin, Norma has had a secret affair with a Roman officer, resulting in the birth of two children. The Italian gentleman then proceeds to seduce another virgin of the temple, who confesses to Norma; the opera ends with the self-sacrifice of Norma. The success of *Norma* was to some extent political; Bellini was an ardent Italian patriot, and the chorus of Druid warriors shouting for the expulsion of the Romans was easily applied to the anti-Austrian ferment of the time. Romanticism in Italy was always patriotic, rather than literary, and the *Risorgimento* owed much to the inspiring strains of Italian opera.

Political opera brings us back to Paris again for Rossini's *Moses in Egypt* (French version, Paris, 1827), and Auber's *Masaniello* (Paris, 1828), a story of the Neapolitan rebellion of 1647. When this opera was produced in 1839 at Brussels, the audience went out into the street and started a revolution of their own which led to the separation of Belgium from Holland. *Masaniello* is one of the first operas with a tragic end; the heroine (who, being dumb, is represented by a *prima ballerina*) leaps from the balcony of the royal palace at Naples into the crater of Vesuvius, a distance of some eight or nine miles.

In 1829 there followed Rossini's masterpiece, *William Tell*. In this huge spectacular opera, full of immense choruses and ballets, like *Fernand Cortez,* Rossini employed all those gifts which had hitherto obtained him facile popularity in a spirit of devout seriousness. *William Tell* is a singers' opera in the sense that it requires magnificent voices and the most accomplished vocal technique, but every effect of virtuosity is concentrated on the drama, which ends with a scene of incomparable grandeur.

After the success of *William Tell*, which was to have been the first of six operas commissioned for Paris, Rossini suddenly retired into private life and wrote no more for the stage. Various reasons have been alleged for this step, but the most probable one was simply bad health, for during the remaining forty years of his life Rossini was always more or less of an invalid.

The new operas for Paris were written by Giacomo Meyerbeer (1791–1864), a Jew from Berlin who had already had some success in Italy as an operatic composer in the manner

66

of Rossini. Meyerbeer has been so much abused by later historians and critics, both as a musician and as a man, that it is worth while stating here that in his younger days he was regarded as an incredibly fascinating and lovable character. Both Weber and Felice Romani (Bellini's librettist), who knew him very intimately, spoke of him in terms of the most ardent affection; they also recorded their gratitude to Meyerbeer's parents, who must have been ideal examples of those cultivated wealthy Jews to whom German musical life has always owed its chief support.

Meyerbeer was not the creator of spectacular political opera; he merely fell in with the taste of his time and followed in the track of Spontini, Auber and Rossini. His personal contribution was chiefly the immense care and thought which he gave to every detail. Even his early Italian operas show this; instead of the empty-looking pages of his contemporaries who seemed always to be writing at top speed and contenting themselves with the most commonplace routine accompaniments, we find an elaborate and ingenious orchestration that may well have caused managers to complain on account of all the extra instruments involved. If Meyerbeer's operas are not much performed today it is very largely because they require gorgeously spectacular settings. Spectacle was what Paris wanted in the 1820s; this was not peculiar to opera, for romantic drama, and before that, melodrama, had shown Parisian audiences what modern machinery could represent.

From the melodrama came the element of the macabre which was conspicuous in Meyerbeer's first opera for Paris, *Robert the Devil*, produced in 1831. The same year saw the production of a comic opera in which the macabre is an essential feature, *Zampa*, by Hérold, now remembered only by its overture. These two operas appear to be the first in which an organ on the stage was utilized; the 'church scene', or something like it, now becomes a characteristic feature of romantic opera. Before the French Revolution anything of the kind would have been forbidden in Catholic countries, although England had had church scenes on the stage since the days of Shakespeare.

Meyerbeer's most successful opera was *The Huguenots* (1836), to a stirring historical libretto by the accomplished playwright Scribe. It is only recently that this work seems to have fallen out of the repertory. *The Prophet* (1849), dealing with the story of John of Leyden and the Anabaptists at Münster in 1535, was rather conventional in style; its most notable features were the coronation march, long a favourite with English organists, the skating ballet, and the magnificent part of Fidés, the Prophet's mother, sung by Mme Viardot-Garcia, which served as a model for Verdi's Azucena. Last came *L'Africaine*, begun in 1838, but never bought out until after the composer's death (1865), which is musically Meyerbeer's best work and contains many scenes of great nobility and beauty.

We must now turn back to Meyerbeer's youthful friend, Carl Maria von Weber (1786–1826), who is the outstanding figure of the German romantic movement. The musical aspects of what is known in general cultural history as the Romantic Movement are very difficult to analyse. Opera is a very important department of romantic music, because opera, with its insistence on human passion and emotion, has always been the place in which the *emotional* language of music has first found utterance. It is opera which has shown composers the way to fill their abstract music with poetry and feeling; the works of Haydn, Mozart and Beethoven alone are sufficient demonstration of this. Yet if we try to define what constitutes the romantic element in the music of an opera we shall find ourselves in perpetual confusion. Pick out any detail that strikes you as romantic in an opera by Weber, and you will almost certainly be able to find the same thing, or the germ of it, in Handel or Rameau, Méhul or Rossini. It is not a matter of plagiary in the least, hardly even of subconscious memory; it is simply that the stream of music is continuous. If Weber is obviously indebted to Rossini, so is Rossini to Mozart, and Mozart to someone else.

It is necessary to remind the reader of this, because many writers have seemed to suggest either that Weber is descended musically straight from Beethoven and Mozart or that he is a genius without musical ancestry. We have already seen that there is something in even early Beethoven which cannot be accounted for by descent from Mozart and Haydn; and it is still more obvious that there is an even wider gulf between

Beethoven and Weber. That gulf can only be filled by the now forgotten French and Italian opera composers, who had the same sort of influence on Weber as they had on his less fortunate though more gifted contemporary Schubert.

Weber left three important operas: *Der Freischütz* (Berlin, 1821), *Euryanthe* (Vienna, 1823), and *Oberon* (London, 1826). Not one of these is really familiar to English audiences. *Der Freischütz* is still one of the most popular of all operas in Germany; it is the favourite opera to which to take children, only rivalled by *Hänsel and Gretel*. *Oberon,* in various rearrangements by other hands, makes an occasional appearance at the larger theatres; quite recently (December, 1938) it was revived in the most unexpected place – Rome. *Euryanthe* has become a sort of 'museum opera' like Mozart's *Idomeneo*, put on the stage by devoted enthusiasts at extremely rare intervals and then regretfully consigned again to the shelves of the library.

The title *Der Freischütz* is impossible to translate directly into English; it means a man who shoots with magic bullets. The scene is laid in a Bohemian village in the seventeenth century, though in these days no one could consider the opera anything except typically German. A young forester who has had bad luck in a shooting contest is persuaded by a depraved comrade to join him in casting magic bullets with the help of the Devil; the result of this is that he manages to shoot his own sweetheart, who is miraculously preserved from death in order that the opera may come to a moderately happy end. Weber has been popularly credited with a good deal that he did not himself invent; Spohr, Schubert and E. T. A. Hoffmann (the hero of Offenbach's *Tales of Hoffman*, who was a real person, and a composer of operas as well as a novelist) had all written operas dealing with some sort of devilry, and Weber was well acquainted with them. The immediate success of *Der Freischütz* was due largely to the fact that it combines a great variety of obvious attractions. It has peasant humour as well as ghostly terrors. To us of today the scene in the Wolf's Glen where the magic bullets are cast is still marvellously exciting, with its *crescendo* of horrors vividly illustrated by continuous music, interrupted only by fragments of spoken dialogue that seem the more horrible because they are not sung. But to German audiences the opera has become endeared by its 'village' atmosphere and the rustic simplicity of the songs and dances which suggest it; it is so essentially German that a foreigner inevitably feels himself a little strange to it.

With *Euryanthe* Weber set out to elevate romantic opera to the dignity of the old court operas. There is no spoken dialogue, and the music is continuous. Much of it is very picturesque, but the story is terribly confused, besides being full of unnecessary complications which are never made clear to the audience. Weber is always said to have had a genius for the stage ; but he seems to have had little understanding for the gradual unfolding of a drama, though he had a very quick eye to the sort of momentary theatrical effect that provokes applause. Like all Germans he had more feeling for the orchestra than for the human voice; it is not that he gives the singers impossible passages to sing, but just at the moment when they ought to have their greatest opportunity he snatches the whole music away from them and gives his climax to the orchestra.

Oberon is an opera which ought to be revived in England with the original English dialogue. Weber was invited to compose an opera for London after the success of an English adaptation of *Der Freischütz*. He knew no English and naturally had no idea of what London was expecting. Planché, the author of the libretto, conceived of opera merely as an excuse for scenery and pageantry. In spite of this, *Oberon* contains by far the best music that Weber ever wrote; the famous overture transports us at once into the realm of fairy-tale, and every scene has an extraordinary originality and picturesqueness.

The lives of the great musicians are seldom interesting, except as illustrating the development of their music and the times in which they lived. Weber is a striking exception, for the erratic circumstances of his life remind one almost of Casanova, and he had every temptation to become nothing more than an adventurer. But nothing has ever been recorded about Weber that was in the slightest degree discreditable to him; on the contrary, he is known to have had a very happy domestic life, and he was also a man of devoted and lifelong friendships. We can, however, understand that the social life of his youth left its traces on his musical inspiration. The final achievement of *Oberon* may justly be ascribed to genius; it is irresistible in its impulse and fascination and it is intensely personal and individual. All the same, it can be analysed and a study of contemporary opera will show us clearly how much of Weber's style was derived from Cherubini and Méhul, Paer and Rossini. We can see Weber as the brilliant and attractive young man, delighting his friends in smart society by sitting down to the pianoforte after an evening of French or Italian opera, and improvising on all the favourite tunes, in the dashing style of his own concertos. Without Weber, there could never have been a Chopin or Liszt, and the best parts of Mendelssohn owe their inspiration to memories of Weber.

CHAPTER FIVE

WAGNER

IF Weber was one of the most attractive human personalities in the history of music, Richard Wagner (1813–83), whose music began where Weber's left off, was one of the most unpleasant as far as his private life was concerned. Wagner was a short man with a large head and a prominent nose and chin; like many short men, he had a great consciousness of his own importance, and was an indefatigable talker. He was a ruthless egotist, and throughout his life regarded other human beings merely in so far as they served the accomplishment of his own purpose. The result of his amazing tenacity was that he became not merely the most striking figure in the history of opera, but also one of the most vital forces in the cultural life of his century.

From childhood he was attracted to the theatre, and he was already writing plays before he had any thought of devoting himself to music. Wagner is the first case of a composer who wrote all his own librettos. His first attempt at opera was *Die Feen* (*The Fairies*) based on a play of Gozzi; it was written in 1833, but never performed until after his death. Next followed *Das Liebesverbot* (*The Ban on Love*), performed once only at Magdeburg in 1836; this is a comic opera in the style of Auber, based on the plot of *Measure for Measure*. It had the reputation of being very licentious, but there is nothing in it that would frighten a modern audience, and the chief tendency of its plot is to throw ridicule on pompous authority. *Rienzi* (Dresden, 1842) is an imitation of Meyerbeer, and is still performed fairly often in Germany. A more original style began to appear in *The Flying Dutchman* (Dresden, 1843), in which Wagner reverted towards the manner of Weber. The opera is a curious mixture of styles, and this is not surprising when we remember that Wagner had been a theatrical conductor for some years and was familiar with all the repertory of the day. French influences are still prominent in *The Flying Dutchman*; Auber was not yet forgotten, and Senta's famous ballad is obviously suggested by the *romance* indispensable to any French comic opera. Her leap from a high rock into the sea is another relic of French tradition.

Tannhäuser came out at Dresden in 1845; in 1849 Wagner became involved in a revolution and had to fly from Germany. He took refuge in Switzerland, and his next opera, *Lohengrin*, was performed for the first time at Weimar in 1850 conducted by Liszt in Wagner's absence. These are the two operas of Wagner best known to the general public and it is difficult to realize now why there should have been such an outcry against Wagner in those days and indeed throughout most of his life.

In these last three works Wagner began to discover the field that was to be peculiarly his own, that of old German legend; it is clear, too, what a difference was made to Wagner's whole outlook on opera by the fact that he was his own librettist instead of having to accept a libretto from someone else. One can see quite easily that Auber, like most of the composers of his time, is setting out to write *an opera*, not to give musical expression to a drama. Opera is already a going concern, with certain regular habitual features, such as songs, duets, choruses, ensembles, etc. The ordinary professional composer of that period did not want to achieve a new form of drama; he wanted success, and that meant doing what somebody else had done before. The problem of the librettist was to find a story that could be utilized to provide all the stock attractions, and the French librettists knew perfectly well how to set to work. So did the Italians on the whole, though when they took French plays as foundations

73

they found some difficulty in converting them into librettos without losing some vital link in the dramatic chain.

Wagner in his first attempts at opera followed traditional lines, and knew as well as any Frenchman what was wanted in the way of a libretto with all the conventionalities. His literary skill gave him a great advantage over other German musicians, for in the early history of German opera it is clear that composers were always severely hampered by the general incompetence of German librettists. In considering the rise of Wagner as an operatic composer we must remember that his career began at a time when Germany possessed an extraordinary wealth of literary genius. The two greatest poets, Goethe and Schiller, had chosen the theatre to be the focus of their creative activity, and they, with the help of various other writers, made the German theatre a temple consecrated to the highest ideals of the German nation, not merely a place of amusement as it was in England, or a battleground of literary cliques as in Paris. This religious devotion to the theatre naturally affected the development of German opera, especially as all German romanticism was inseparably bound up with music. In no other country was literature so conscious of music or music so closely associated with literature. France can show but one outstanding figure – Berlioz – who is a writer as well as a musician; though we must not forget that in an earlier generation Grétry and Lesueur had been men of letters. But in Germany almost every musician of eminence cherished literary ambitions – Weber, Spohr, Schumann, Hoffmann are the conspicuous examples. Later on come Liszt and Cornelius (though Liszt as a rule preferred to write in French); and Mendelssohn, though never a journalist, was certainly a man of literary cultivation. Most of the German poets knew something of music, and it was only natural that the romantic age should be at one and the same time the great period of German lyric poetry and the great age of German song.

Germany in those days was proud to call itself 'the land of poets and thinkers', and Wagner may justly claim to belong to both these categories. A new spirit becomes perceptible in *Lohengrin*, which was the fruit of solitude and meditation, whereas Wagner's previous operas had been written in the thick of professional life. *Lohengrin* looks forward to the last

74

of Wagner's dramas, *Parsifal*; both are concerned with the story of the Holy Grail, and Lohengrin actually informs us at the end of the opera that Parsifal is his father. The French composers of the Revolution had tried curious experiments in writing dramatic instrumental prologues to their operas instead of conventional overtures; but the prelude to *Lohengrin* showed an entirely new sort of theatrical imagination in its very first bars. It is supposed to describe the descent of the Holy Grail to earth and its return to Heaven. Most members of the audience probably know nothing about that and would not much care if they did; but everyone must admit that it is one of the most beautiful pieces of music ever written, and it may well stand as the movement which most perfectly expresses that sense of 'aspiration' which was characteristic of the whole life and thought of the nineteenth century.

From this moment onwards Wagner's whole life was dedicated to the accomplishment of an ideal – 'the work of art of the future' that was to unite in itself all the arts in the service of the musical drama. Wagner never stopped to consider practicalities in the theatre. His new dramas were to be full of things which were contrary to all tradition and had never been done before; these things have by now become more or less normal and accepted.

In his later operas Wagner goes his own way. Although he habitually wrote his libretto complete before composing the music, he certainly had a good many of his musical ideas germinating in his mind while putting the words into shape, so that we can regard these operas as simultaneous conceptions of poetry and music. And we must remember, too, that Wagner never lost contact with the concert room. Italian composers of the time seem to have gone on composing operas as if they never came across any other kind of music; one might easily imagine that Bellini and Donizetti never heard a classical symphony in their lives. Wagner, on the other hand, was keenly interested in concert conducting, and in fact it was he who started the outlook on orchestral music which led to the modern idolization of the star conductor. Hence he was able to absorb into the technique of the theatre the musical methods of Beethoven's symphonies and other classical works. Purely operatic experience might well teach him how to present characters on the stage and how to achieve obvious theatrical effects. From Beethoven, more than from anyone else, he learned what one might call the technique of rumination upon the events of the drama.

It was said a few pages back that Beethoven, in *Fidelio,* often seems to forget the actual characters on the stage and lose himself in the contemplation of a moral idea. Wagner does the same thing, but with more deliberate intention and with a new technique of his own. This could not become possible until and after Beethoven had perfected the process which in sonatas and symphonies is called *development*; in was only this technique which made it possible for Wagner to drop the old system of isolated songs with opportunities for applause at the end, and create a continuous style of music which allowed no thought of applause, not even a moment of respite until the end of each act. This forced audiences, as Wagner was consciously determined to achieve, into a new attitude towards opera. It was no longer possible to drop in and go away just as one pleased, hear a particular singer and not bother about the rest; an opera had to be taken seriously, and the audience had to give themselves up to it, abandoning all independence of personality like a patient submitting to an anaesthetic. And this applied not only to the audience; the singers and the orchestra, the scene-shifters, too, were compelled to make the same utter self-surrender and become no more than atoms absorbed into the one mighty stream of the composer's imagination. The doors are shut, the lights go down, the conductor raises his stick; and from that moment everyone is the slave of the music. There can be no waiting while a scene is being changed; lighting and machinery must function like instruments in the score, with the same precision. We are so accustomed to all this nowadays that we can hardly imagine what operatic conditions were like before Wagner; yet those whose memories go back to the 1890s will not have forgotten the indignation of old *habitués* at Covent Garden when it was proposed to darken the auditorium for *The Ring* and close the doors to late arrivals.

A modern German history of music gives a list of some six

hundred German operas produced between about 1830 and 1900; hardly a single one has remained in the ordinary German repertory, apart from a few comic operas and musical comedies of the 1840s which are still popular in their own country, though little known outside. Throughout the whole of Wagner's lifetime the German theatres were dependent mainly on French and Italian operas, just as they were in the days of Mozart, and indeed right up to 1900 and later certain old French comic operas survived in Germany which had long been shelved in France. It is necessary to insist on this in order that the reader may realize the strength of the opposition to Wagner and the immensity of the conquest which he finally achieved.

The chronology of Wagner's later works is very confusing, as he had the habit of beginning a drama and making sketches for it, and then taking up something else, leaving the first work to be completed many years afterwards. The following table gives the important dates:

	First sketches	*Begun*	*Ended*	*First performed*
Tristan and Isolde	—	1857	1859	1865, Munich
The Mastersingers	1845	1861	1867	1868, Munich
The Ring of the Nibelung: Poem begun 1848, finished 1852				
1. *The Rhinegold*	—	1853	1854	1869, Munich
2. *The Valkyrie*	—	1854	1856	1870, Munich
3. *Siegfried*	—	1854	1871	1876, Bayreuth
4. *The Twilight of the Gods*	—	1870	1874	1876, Bayreuth
Parsifal	1857	1876	1882	1882, Bayreuth

The most important of these works is the great tetralogy of *The Ring.* Wagner's first idea was to write one drama only, to be called *Siegfried's Death,* founded on an episode from the ancient legendary epic of Germany, the *Nibelungenlied.* But he found that the story required so much explanation that he would have to write another opera as a prologue to it; and that led to another and yet another, so that the four dramas of *The Ring* came to be written in the inverse order of their natural sequence. During the years occupied in this work Wagner's mind underwent changes, so that the last of the four is much more like an old-fashioned opera than the first.

The suicide of the heroine, by throwing herself (on horseback) on to the burning funeral pyre of her husband, at once reminds us of Auber's Fenella, who jumps into the crater of Vesuvius, and Halévy's Jewess who jumps into a cauldron of boiling oil; and the final destruction of the palace by fire looks back to Cherubini's *Lodoiska* (1791), an opera quite often performed in Germany in Wagner's younger days. And Hagen's dive into the overflowing Rhine also has its parallel in various old French operas; Wagner, with his usual eye to grandoise stage effect, merely combined three stock operatic endings in one.

Apart from these relics of an earlier convention, *The Ring* breaks away from all traditional systems, though one can still find alterations of recitative and air – that is, of passages which are mainly declamatory contrasted with lyrical episodes. Wagnerian music-drama professes to follow the free form of the poem, but Wagner was far too good a musician to let his music become chaotic and formless, and he clearly laid out his poems with a view to their musical form. It was for this purpose that he adopted an entirely new metrical system, derived from early medieval German poetry, based on alliteration, and employing very short lines instead of the long rhymed lines which make *Lohengrin* so tedious in general effect. English poetry had made use of alliterative verse in the early fifteenth century (e.g. *Piers Plowman*), but it does not lend itself easily to modern English, and translations of Wagner have often provoked smiles.

It was a terrible shock to Wagner's early audiences to find that he had abolished not only separate airs and 'numbers', but also practically all choruses and all ensembles. It is only in *The Mastersingers* and *Parsifal* that the chorus has a really important part. What Wagner wanted to get rid of was the conventionality of the old-fashioned chorus, who did nothing but stand in a row and bawl music that sounds like the middle parts of a brass band. In the days of Bellini and Donizetti no chorus singers were expected to read at sight; they learned everything by ear. They were miserably paid and amounted to little more than supers; and it is very noticeable that in all these old operas, French, German or Italian, the chorus is almost exclusively male. Women are not kept out altogether, but the amount they have to sing is very small compared with that of the male choruses; and we learn from Weber that in his day it was extremely difficult to obtain women chorus singers at all. When Weber conducted Spontini's *La Vestale* at Dresden, he had to get boys from a church choir school (the very school which Wagner attended as a boy) to take the parts of Vestal virgins.

Living for so many years in exile, away from all contact with the German theatre, Wagner became more and more obsessed with the grandeur of his own ideas. In 1861 he had paid a visit to Paris, where he had had the humiliating experience of seeing his *Tannhäuser* hissed off the stage; this was quite enough to set him against France for many years, although in his last days he was very devoutly worshipped by a small group of French admirers, most of them extremely distinguished people. As *The Ring* grew ever larger in his conception, he began to see that this would never be realized unless he could build himself a theatre of his own, a place set apart, a shrine of pilgrimage. Thanks to King Ludwig II of Bavaria, who took him under his protection in 1864, the idea of a Festival Theatre became a practical possibility. The King's own wish had been to build it at Munich, but Wagner's position in Munich had become impossible in 1865 and he found it necessary to leave that city and go back to Switzerland. Wagner finally decided that his theatre should be built at Bayreuth, a little town not very far from Nürnberg, which had formerly been the capital of a diminutive principality. The town authorities welcomed the scheme and the cost of the theatre was defrayed mostly by private subscripion among Wagner's friends and admirers. It was opened in August, 1876, with the first complete performance of *The Ring*.

The Ring has now passed into the stock repertory of every large theatre; it can be seen in Paris, London or Milan every year. But it was a long time before even the German theatres had the courage to undertake so vast a task, and in old days a performance even at Bayreuth was a rare event and an unforgettable experience. If we see *The Ring* today, we see it just as one among many other operas, probably with the same singers, the same orchestra, and in the same theatre – wherever it may happen to be – with its boxes and galleries all round and its invariable mass of gilding all about the proscen-

79

ium, which even in a darkened house glitters in the light reflected from the desks of the orchestra. At Bayreuth, one was there to hear Wagner and for no other purpose. The theatre stood apart from the town, on a hill by itself; before each act began, a group of brass instruments on the terrace sounded a fanfare from the opera. Inside the theatre everything was as plain and neutral as possible; there were no galleries at the sides, only rows and rows of gradually rising seats, all facing the stage directly, so that one was hardly conscious of one's neighbours. The orchestra was in a sunken pit, so that the players – and the conductor, too, thank goodness – were completely invisible. There was nothing to see but the stage. The scenic designs of those days were too strictly realistic for modern taste, but they were executed with astonishing skill, and no other theatre of that time could approach Bayreuth in stagecraft. Everything combined to take one away from the ordinary world, even from the ordinary world of music; one's whole receptive personality was concentrated on the stage and on the product of Wagner's imagination. Surrender was complete, not only to Wagner's work of art but to every principle of Wagner's outlook on the relation of art to life.

At the present day there is a considerable feeling of reaction against Wagner and all that he stood for. Music has moved on and life has become filled with all sorts of new distractions. It is perhaps natural that many of us should say we have no time to listen to these slow-moving and interminable histories of primitive Teutonic gods and heroes. *The Ring* has ceased to be a rare experience, and producers take less and less trouble about it. But if you are young, and have never seen it, it may still be one of the great experiences of your life. If you have seen it so often that you are interested only in comparing one singer or conductor with another, or in criticizing divergences from orthodox tradition, then it is time you made up your mind to relegate *The Ring* to the museum of memory, and never go to see it again.

As regards *Tristan* and *The Mastersingers*, most people are inclined to love one and hate the other, whichever it may be; it is a question of personal temperament. *Tristan* is all chromatics, and there are many people who find it 'morbid', 'decadent' and utterly unbearable; *The Mastersingers* has always been the favourite of those clean-minded English people who want music to be 'healthy' above everything. It is a testimony to Wagner's greatness that such criticisms should still be made now that Wagner has been dead for over fifty years. Surely it would be better to let him pass over to the realm of the classics, and listen to *Tristan* simply as a work of beauty. The same applies to *The Mastersingers*, especially for us English people who are not particularly interested in its essential Germanism. In Germany this opera has become a national symbol, and even in this country conductors are apt to forget that its composer deliberately entitled it a comic opera.

In *Parsifal*, his last work, Wagner demanded an even more complete surrender of his audience than ever before, and it was his wish that *Parsifal* should never be performed outside his own theatre at Bayreuth. As long as it was protected by copyright law, it did remain the exclusive possession of Bayreuth; but on 24 December 1903 a performance was given at the Metropolitan Opera House, New York. Paris heard it for the first time on 1 January 1914 and the first performance in England followed a month later. In Germany *Parsifal* is generally performed on Good Friday; in former times theatres were always closed on that day, but *Parsifal* is considered as a sufficiently sacred work, and it is sure to fill the house.

An opera which represented on the stage a ceremony that was practically the same thing as the Catholic Mass was naturally the subject of much discussion from the first. Some devout people thought it blasphemous, but the general trend of opinion has been to accept the work in the spirit in which it was supposed to have been written, and to regard it as a solemn confession of faith. Other people, perhaps not much concerned about faith, have felt offended by *Parsifal* as being an insincere exploitation of religion by a man whose whole life had stood for the very opposite of that doctrine of renunciation preached in the opera.

Wagner's literary works, and his interpretations of his own operas, may have been a valuable advertisement for them in his own time, but most people of today will feel that they prefer to think of him as a musician and as little else. The days of

Wagnerian controversy are over; the 'music of the future' has become the music of the past. We can enjoy *Parsifal* and derive spiritual benefit from it, whether we believe in these things or not, and it is a matter of no artistic moment whether Wagner himself believed in them. There can still be no doubt that *Parsifal*, like *Tristan*, is a work of extraordinary musical beauty; let us surrender to that and concentrate our minds upon it.

Wagner's influence on the form of the operatic libretto, and his influence on the purely musical aspects of opera will be discussed in a later chapter. His political and philosophical views do not concern us, although he often believed that they were intimately connected with his music. As time passes on, all these things, once matters of acute controversy, become forgotten; they are manifestations of their own period, and the present age is content to leave them to the makers of research dissertations. Poetry and music remain, though we have to recognize that the heat of inspiration dies down, and the music of the romantics is no longer as exciting and overwhelming as it was in its own day.

Apart from the creation of these individual works of art, Wagner, through his writings and through his own personal influence, has converted the musical world, or a good part of it, to something like a new outlook on music in general. It may be that he was mistaken in supposing that the modern world could ever recover the attitude of ancient Greece to the religious aspect of musical drama, but he certainly induced it to take music, and especially opera, far more seriously than it had ever done before. When one looks back over the musical history of his century, and the developments which brought Germany the musical leadership of Europe, it is astonishing to think that opera played so small a part in them. What did Beethoven leave us in opera? One work, and that reserved for veneration rather than full-bloodedly enjoyed. Schubert? A dozen failures, the very existence of which is unknown to the millions who can hum the themes of the *Unfinished Symphony*. Schumann and Mendelssohn made timid experiments; and Brahms had not even the courage for that. Weber is the only name besides Wagner, and we have seen what his production amounted to. Besides, in the orthodox world of music, Weber was sometimes regarded as not quite on a level with the rest of the great German masters; his symphonies, concertos and sonatas were thought showy rather than profound, and his church music was considered operatic. 'Operatic' was in fact always a word of disparagement, almost of moral disapproval; and if Wagner had been an Englishman, he would probably have used it himself in that sense.

The serious musicians of the nineteenth century turned away from opera, as if it was an unclean trade; and there are music-lovers who still maintain this point of view. Many hard things have been said about Wagner, and as far as his private life was concerned, he deserved a good many of them; but it could never be said of Wagner that he was not a serious-minded musician. He had faith in himself, and courage, which was what most of his contemporaries, however distinguished, had not. It was mainly owing to the influence of Wagner that a certain standard of artistic integrity has been brought into most of the great opera houses and many of the small ones; we owe to him the spirit of team-work and ensemble, of devotion to the work of art on the part of every single member of the company and staff. That was the spirit of Bayreuth, and from Bayreuth it has spread all over the world.

We owe it to Wagner that the auditorium is darkened as a matter of course during a performance, that the doors are shut and late-comers made to wait outside; we owe it to him that a soft prelude is heard in silence, and applause reserved for the end of an act. It may be replied that there are still many theatres where silence is not maintained, and that there are also many operas still in the repertory which suffer from uncomfortable moments when the applause which the composer expected is so reverently restrained. Nevertheless, the Wagnerian attitude to performance is on the whole an advantage to an opera of any style or period, for it gives us a chance of concentrating our attention on the drama itself.

These points of social observance are trivial compared with the fundamental principle which was at the base of all Wagner's doctrines and labours – that a work of art should be a spiritual experience, and that the summit of such experience could only be attained in the theatre, where all the arts were united in this sublime act of worship. There can be no doubt that Bayreuth in the past did bring to many people of various nationalities a spiritual experience such as Wagner envisaged. It is obvious that such experiences can seldom be repeated, and it is hardly credible that any human being can live in a perpetual state of mystical ecstasy, especially in the modern world of practical life. Besides, our sense of humour – at any rate in England – is always breaking in, and at the most enraptured moments the stage cat is sure to take the footlights. Every individual has to decide for himself whether scepticism or credulity is the preferable state of mind; but anyone who has ever known the complete surrender of the soul to music and drama in the theatre will never enter an opera house without at least some faint hope that the experience may be renewed.

Many years passed before the next generation of German composers began to divide Wagner's heritage between them. Imitation Wagner was practicable only for theatres which had adopted the machinery of Bayreuth, and that sort of stage reform was naturally a long and gradual process, corresponding to the rate at which managers and conductors resolved to put *The Ring* on their own stages. The attempts to rival or to surpass *The Ring* were none of them successful, and musicians soon realized that new directions must be taken. Wagner himself seemed to point many different ways, and his followers could be grouped in families, according as they pursued the 'hearty' style of *The Mastersingers,* the erotics of *Tristan,* the morbid religiosity and exploitation of suffering derived from *Parsifal,* or attempted to scale the monumental heights of *The Ring.* The most successful of the post-Wagnerians did none of these things; he took a fairy-tale in the style of the brothers Grimm and a handful of nursery songs and summed up all that is most delightful and lovable in German romantic legend in *Hänsel and Gretel* (1893), a children's opera which at this moment is probably more popular in England than in the land of its origin.

CHAPTER SIX

VERDI – GOUNOD – PUCCINI – THE RUSSIANS

WAGNER, though not born to affluence, belonged to the educated classes; he went to a famous school where he was taught Latin and Greek, and eventually matriculated at the University of Leipzig. Giuseppe Verdi (1813–1901), born in the same year as Wagner, came of the humblest peasant stock, and had no chance of literary education until he had already made a name for himself in the theatre. He entered upon his career at a moment when Italian opera was at its lowest; Rossini had retired from the stage, Bellini was dead, and Donizetti was the victim of mental disease. There was little at first to distinguish the young Verdi from the crowd of mediocrities whose names and works are almost completely forgotten, even in Italy, and Verdi himself had no idea of writing operas except with a view to immediate popular success. Contemporary critics found these early works coarse and brutal in style, well enough suited to a new generation of singers who had large and heavy voices but no refinement or elegance of technique such as had been characteristic of the great interpreters of Bellini. Verdi in his youth had had a good deal of practice in writing music for a brass band in his native town of Busseto, and the brass band style is very conspicuous in all these early operas. Many of them in fact have a real brass band on the stage, or behind the scenes, as well as the normal orchestra, and it invariably plays in the cheap military style of the day, whatever the dramatic situation may be and whatever the period represented. The most fortunate thing for Verdi at this early stage of his career was that his music somehow became associated with the patriotic movement that was eventually to expel the Austrians from Italian territory and unite the whole country under the House of Savoy. Verdi himself always professed to stand completely aside from politics, but considering the perpetual trouble that he had with the Austrian censorship over almost every one of his early operas, it is not surprising that he should have rejoiced in the opportunity of stimulating that movement by the impulsive ardour of his melodies. He had from the first a remarkable melodic talent; for many generations his tunes were the favourites of the barrel-organs. At the present day, when these melodies have become too old-fashioned for the streets, Verdi's early operas have enjoyed a surprising revival, and much ingenuity has been devoted by modern conductors and producers to rehabilitating operas which in Verdi's own time were comparative failures.

Verdi's first important opera was *Nabucco* (*Nebuchadnezzar*), produced at Milan in 1842; it was revived a few years ago at Florence. Its chief attraction was the touching chorus of Hebrew captives singing a paraphrase of the Psalm, 'By the waters of Babylon', which in the original production had started the association of Verdi with the *Risorgimento*. Another fine chorus that was adopted by the patriots occurred in *I Lombardi* (*The Lombards at the First Crusade,* Milan, 1843) when the Crusaders catch their first sight of Jerusalem. The modern Englishman can hardly conceive what obstacles were placed in Verdi's way by the government authorities, whether they were Austrian, as at Milan and Venice, Papal in Rome, or Neapolitan. Madame Pasta, when she came to London in 1833, told Lady Morgan that she had narrowly escaped imprisonment at Naples because she had pronounced the world *libertà* on the stage. The censorship forbade anything that could be interpreted as bringing ridicule or odium on authority, on kings or emperors of any age; any allusion to the Church was dangerous, and the use of any word that had sacred associations; and any representation of a conspiracy was utterly impossible. In the days of Metastasio the actual regulations may very likely have been more severe, but they did not matter, for it would never have occurred to any librettist to offend against them. The tyranny under which Verdi had to suffer was peculiarly annoying to poets and composers who wanted to make operas out of French romantic dramas.

Ernani (Venice, 1844) marks Verdi's first contact with Victor Hugo, and *Macbeth* (Florence, 1847) his first approach to Shakespeare. *Ernani* is still acted in Italy, and *Macbeth* had a spectacular revival in Berlin a few years ago. The first opera which showed Verdi's real dramatic genius was *Rigoletto* (Venice, 1851), on a libretto taken from Victor Hugo's play *Le Roi s'amuse*. Hugo's play had caused a scandal at its first production in 1832, and it is quite possible that Verdi chose it for this very reason, much as Mozart chose *Le Mariage de Figaro*, because it was a play that had been forbidden, ostensibly on moral grounds; as an Italian opera, it might possibly be allowed to pass. There were the usual obstructions; but after the historical King of France had been transformed into an imaginary Duke of Mantua, the libretto was permitted. *Rigoletto* is a drama of violent passions and what are called strong situations; it attracted Verdi because the hero of the play, instead of being the usual obviously sympathetic character, a principal tenor and nothing more, was a creature of complex emotions, externally hideous, and attractive only in the more secret side of his personality.

Two more operas came out in 1853, *Il Trovatore* at Rome and *La Traviata* at Venice; the first was an immediate success, the second a disastrous failure. *Il Trovatore* continued the direction of *Rigoletto;* it is based on a Spanish drama that shows the influence of Victor Hugo's sensational manner, but has a peculiar lyricism of its own. The Spanish play was designed as a *poetical* play in which poetry justified the violence of passion. For this reason it was appropriate for an opera, and now that Verdi's early works have taken on a certain patina of classicality, we can accept the absurdities of the story for the sake of the emotions which the opera presents with an irresistible fervour and intensity.

In *La Traviata* Verdi tried the experiment of setting to music a tragic drama of contemporary life. Here again he took a well-known play as a basis, *La Dame aux Camélias* of Alexandre Dumas *fils*, which he had seen acted in Paris in 1852. The failure of the opera on its first production has been ascribed to the incapacity of the singers, and more particularly to the corpulence of the consumptive heroine; but Mr Bonavia is probably right in supposing that the real reason for the disaster was the refusal of an audience to tolerate opera – and tragedy, too – in modern dress. The result was that for many years *La Traviata* was always put back to some remoter century, although it was customary for the heroine to wear gowns in the very latest fashion and as many diamonds as she possessed. Under such conditions it is not surprising that serious musicians regarded the opera with utter contempt. Gemma Bellincioni, who in Verdi's own opinion was the ideal Traviata, began about 1904 to sing the opera in a crinoline dress; not till then was the crinoline considered as anything but ridiculous. Her interpretation of the part – she was a woman of striking beauty and a truly great actress – was unspeakably moving; and in recent years *La Traviata* has come to be regarded as a serous work, to be performed with care and dignity.

La Traviata is of great historical importance, because it is the first successful attempt at an operatic treatment of domestic tragedy. It was not actually the first, for it was preceded by two other operas of Verdi, *Luisa Miller* (Naples, 1849), founded on Schiller's play, *Kabale und Liebe*, and *Stiffelio* (Trieste, 1850), which from Mr Francis Toye's description of the libretto must have been something like a play by Ibsen. *Luisa Miller* was revived not long ago in Germany; *Stiffelio* was discarded by Verdi himself and the music used for another forgotten opera, *Aroldo* (Rimini, 1857). We have seen how from the very beginning opera was always expected to deal with passions on the heroic plane or else to be frankly comic; and we have seen further how this comic opera became more and more sentimental until it developed into romantic opera, and in this form came to inherit the throne of the long-dead *opera seria*. These three operas of Verdi on tragic stories from ordinary life might be considered as a return to the style of Paer about 1800, but there is this difference, that the older type of opera includes definitely comic (*buffo*) parts, and is always brought to a happy end, whereas Verdi's *bourgeois* operas are entirely serious and end in unmistakable tragedy.

Verdi throughout his life kept in touch with Paris, although he had no great love for that city. *Rigoletto* shows clearly the influence of *Robert the Devil,* and it was through contemporary French opera rather than through Wagner that Verdi gradually educated himself to higher ideals than those of his youth. In 1855 he was commissioned to write a French opera for Paris; this was *Les Vêpres Siciliennes,* in which he seemed to be doing his best to imitate Meyerbeer. His next important work was *Un Ballo in Maschera* (*A Masked Ball,* Rome, 1859), which is still performed in various countries, though not very often. Its libretto brought Verdi into the usual trouble with the censorship, and the story to which the music was finally attached is the most ridiculous imaginable. But the opera contains some magnificent music, and it is further noteworthy as combining distinctly comic elements with the most gruesome tragedy.

Verdi had a keen eye for stage effect, but he had little power of judging a libretto as a whole, though we must make some allowance for the way in which almost every one of his earlier operas was hacked about in the process of censoring. He wanted startling situations, and above all things he wanted strongly drawn characters, like Lady Macbeth or Rigoletto – characters, that is, whom he could paint with his unfailing vividness and his ruthless sincerity of expression. *Un Ballo in Maschera* suffered not only from an absurd story, but from infelicities of phrase which have become proverbial in Italy.

Two more operas of Verdi, which have been recently revived at the Old Vic and Sadler's Wells, were *La Forza del*

Destino (*The Force of Destiny*, St Petersburg, 1862), and *Don Carlos* (Paris, 1867). Both of these suffer from excessive length, and from Verdi's inability to see a story as a whole, though both contain fine scenes and genuinely impressive music. A change of style was coming over Verdi's entire production; he still pursued the ideal of direct stage effect, but he had shaken off the vulgarity which disfigured his early works, and acquired a new sense of dignity. His complete mastery of stage effect was admirably exhibited in *Aïda* (Cairo, 1871), composed for the ceremonial opening of the Suez Canal. The outline of the libretto was prepared by Mariette, an Egyptologist in the service of the Khedive; it was made into an Italian libretto by Ghislanzoni, but Verdi himself kept a constant watch over it and many of the most effective details were suggested by Verdi himself. The story, the scene of which is laid in ancient Egypt, is simple and clear, a great contrast to the complicated plots of Verdi's previous operas. The main function of *Aïda* was to provide a magnificent spectacular entertainment, and it achieves this object to perfection; but the characters, in spite of their legendary antiquity, are thoroughly human and real in their conduct and emotions, and there are indeed few operas which make so direct and convincing an appeal. *Aïda*, from a manager's point of view, is one of the most useful operas in the repertory; it will suit almost any kind of theatre. It can stand the most ostentatious magnificence that Paris or Milan expend on it, and it is within the capacities of houses which dare not risk the grandeurs of either Meyerbeer or Wagner, for the music itself has a quality of grandeur that can make us forget the economy of a modest production. And behind all this façade of sumptuousness there is a wonderful tenderness and sincerity of human feeling.

In 1862 Verdi made his first contact with the poet and composer Arrigo Boito (1842–1918); he had written the words for a cantata which Verdi set to music for the London Exhibition. Verdi, however, seems to have had no great personal regard for Boito, perhaps owing to Boito's ardent admiration for Wagner; and Boito, as a subtle-minded intellectual, had been repelled rather than attracted by Verdi's earlier works. In 1865 he made a spectacular failure with his own attempt to turn both parts of Goethe's *Faust* into an opera – *Mefisto-fele*; and though that opera was revised later and is now one of the honoured classics of the Italian stage, it was not the kind of music that would make a favourable impression on Verdi. None the less, some of Verdi's friends saw that Boito was just the kind of poet whom Verdi now needed as a collaborator, and in 1879 they were brought together with a suggestion that had not emanated from either of them – that they should write an opera on Shakespeare's *Othello*. The project took a long time to mature, and *Otello* did not make its appearance until 1887, four years after the death of Wagner at Venice. That death had made a deep impression on Verdi. He had never met Wagner, and he had always much resented any suggestion that his own music had been influenced by Wagner. In 1871 *Lohengrin* had been performed at Bologna – the first Wagner opera ever heard in Italy; Verdi was present, and the vocal score which he took with him still exists, with his pencil comments in the margins. He was ready to admire Wagner's music, but he had no use for Wagner's theories, and he was firmly convinced that Wagner was a dangerous influence for Italian composers. Wagner made up his mind about Verdi in quite early days, and seems never to have taken the slightest interest in him.

The first collaboration of Verdi and Boito in the theatre was a revision of *Simone Boccanegra,* first composed in 1857, when it was a complete failure; in 1881 Boito remodelled the libretto of Piave, and Verdi rewrote much of the music, cutting out its old-fashioned vulgarities and making the music more continuous. Even then it had no success in Italy, but it was a good deal taken up in Germany during the great Verdi revival of the 1920s. Its first performance in England was in 1948 at Sadler's Wells (in English), where it has had a remarkable popular success, in spite of a most gloomy story.

The death of Wagner left Verdi in complete possession of the operatic field. *Otello* puzzled the critics, and to accuse Verdi of Wagnerism was an easy way of concealing their own inability to understand the change that had gradually taken place in Verdi's methods and style. But the germ of the new style was plainly apparent in *Rigoletto* and the new opera was the logical development of it, reached step by step through the intermediate operas.

What seemed 'Wagnerian' to the critics of 1887 was that *Otello* is much more continuous than any of Verdi's previous operas; Verdi was not so meticulous as Wagner was about avoiding definite stops in the course of a scene, but generally speaking the music runs on without any obvious breaks for applause. Another thing was that the words were on a high literary level, a close translation of Shakespeare as far as possible, and there was no more of that senseless repetition and distortion of literary rhythms that disfigured *Trovatore* and the earlier operas. The orchestra was handled with much greater skill, and there was more development of instrumental themes; Verdi had certainly learned much from Wagner as to technical methods, but after all those methods came originally from Beethoven, whom he had studied all his life. The fundamental difference between Verdi and Wagner lay in their mental outlook on opera. Wagner was always more interested in the orchestra than in the singers; he imagined his characters as emerging from the orchestra, created, as one might say, by the imagination of the orchestra, which was the real expression of his own imagination. He planned his theatre so that the orchestra pit whould form what he called a 'mystic gulf' between the audience and the stage – to remove the singers from the audience rather than to bring them nearer. Verdi's conception of opera was the exact opposite of this. Italian theatres all have enormous aprons to their stages; in some of them the space in front of the curtain is large enough to accommodate a grand pianoforte and some dozen players when concerts are given in the theatre. In old days it was a matter of course that the singers should come down to the footlights to sing their songs; and the orchestra and conductor were there solely for the purpose of accompanying them. Verdi certainly accepted this view of opera, and whereas Wagner wanted to make his characters as unreal and mysterious as possible, Verdi always concentrated on intensifying their reality. That is why, even in his Shakespearean operas, he invariably makes the singers and not the instruments the vehicles of his inmost thought.

After *Otello* it was hardly expected that Verdi would write another opera; but in 1889 Boito suggested to him the subject of Falstaff, and in 1893 the opera of *Falstaff* was brought out at Milan. It was an astonishing achievement for a man of eighty, and although humorous characters had appeared now and then in earlier operas, the mere fact of Verdi's writing a comic opera was enough to startle the musical world. The first performance of *Falstaff*, like that of *Otello*, was surrounded with every possible sort of publicity, although there was nothing that Verdi himself hated more; but in point of fact it took a great many years for either of these operas to establish themselves in popular favour. For a long time they were given more often in Germany than in Italy, though even there they appealed only to a limited circle. In recent years *Falstaff* has become a really popular success in England; the first Italian performance was given at Covent Garden in 1894 and in 1896 it was given in English by the students of the Royal College of Music at the Lyceum Theatre under Sir Charles Stanford, who had been present at the *première* in Milan. *Falstaff* is an opera well suited to England, not so much on account of its subject, as because it cannot be made effective without consistent and careful team-work on the part of the chief singers. Team-work is not a characteristic of the Italian stage, where each singer is anxious to get to the front and capture public attention; and although there is plenty of discipline in German theatres, no German conductor can ever be persuaded that the singers are more important than the orchestra, least of all that the work is more important than himself. But in England we still have a delight in singing, and especially in ensemble singing, and English team-work produces a better result in *Falstaff* than magnificent Italian voices.

Falstaff was much more than just a successful opera which is always a source of enjoyment both to the general public and to the trained musician. Wagner, as we now see, was the end of an epoch, and Verdi might well have been an end as well, if he had finished his career with *Otello*. But *Falstaff* was an opera that looked forward to the future, if only that it made musicians realize that comic opera was not dead after all.

We must now go back a little way and pick up the threads of French opera from the time of Meyerbeer. In the background of the operatic world of Paris stood a strange figure – Hector

Berlioz (1803–69), whose position in the history of music has not yet been finally settled. Berlioz was always a man who stood apart, and his contributions to opera have never fitted neatly and happily into any sort of orthodox system, whether the academic system of the history books or the practical one of the great opera houses. English people know him best by his dramatic cantata *Faust*, and after the composer's death *Faust* was sometimes converted into an opera and put on the stage, for which it is not very well suited. His early comic opera *Benvenuto Cellini* (Paris, 1838) belongs to the style of Auber and also of Wagner's *Das Liebesverbot*, but in musical value it is far superior to either Wagner's early comedy or any of Auber's. Berlioz was a devoted admirer of Shakespeare, and his next opera, *Béatrice et Bénédict* (Baden, 1862) was based on *Much Ado About Nothing*; it covers only a portion of Shakespeare's play, but has scenes of great beauty. His most important work was *Les Troyens*, conceived as a whole, but divided into two operas, *La Prise de Troie* (*The Taking of Troy*) and *Les Troyens à Carthage* (*The Trojans at Carthage*). Only the first of these was ever performed in his lifetime (Paris, 1863), and was a disastrous failure. The first performance of the complete work was at Karlsruhe, in German, in 1897. The whole opera was performed for the first time in Great Britain at Glasgow in 1935.

The detractors of Berlioz generally accuse him of extravagance and exaggeration, but these things are not to be found in *Les Troyens*, which is a work of austere nobility and dignity. Berlioz loved Virgil even more than he did Shakespeare, and the libretto of *Les Troyens,* which he wrote himself, is in many places literally translated from the *Aeneid*. It is hardly a work for the ordinary repertory, but it is one of the few operas ever written that really fulfil Wagner's ideal of music and drama combined to create something on a plane far above the normal level of artistic experience. *Les Troyens* is also of historic importance as the first example of 'epic' opera, in which the story of a nation is of profounder significance than the passions of individual characters. The real hero of *Les Troyens* is not Aeneas, but the Trojan host, driven into exile after the fall of their city and ultimately creating a 'new Troy' on the shores of Italy. The first anticipations of epic opera may be seen in Spontini's *Fernand Cortez* and in Meyerbeer's *Les Huguenots*, which has often been called 'a chapter of French history'; later examples are Wagner's *Ring*, Moussorgsky's *Boris Godunov*, and in recent years *Christophe Colomb* and *Bolivar* of Darius Milhaud.

The ordinary repertory of Paris, apart from Meyerbeer, was based chiefly on Auber, and the earlier composers of comic opera such as Boieldieu and Hérold. Auber lived on until 1871, but none of his many operas surpassed *Fra Diavolo* (Paris, 1830), which is one of the most sparkling comic operas ever composed. The latter half of the century saw the birth of several works which were to become popular all over the world. First among these is Gounod's *Faust* (Paris, 1859). Zola said of it that it was 'the music of a voluptuous priest'. There was always something a little sanctimonious about Gounod (1818–93), who in private life was a most devoutly religious man. The operas of this period represent something halfway between grand opera and *opéra-comique*; *Faust* was in fact originally composed as an *opéra-comique* with spoken dialogue. It is the continuation of the type created in *La Traviata* – not that Verdi's opera had so powerful an influence on composers outside Italy, but because a new type of audience was growing up that demanded a certain refinement of sentiment. This is understandable in connexion with the fact that the same period saw the rise of a lower form of musical drama, known on the Continent as operetta, and in England as musical comedy.

This book is not concerned with the study of the lighter entertainments, which have a history of their own and can be subdivided into a number of periods and categories. It is highly probable that many of the comic operas of remoter days, those of Pergolesi and Galuppi for instance, as well as their French contemporaries, held approximately the same place in public estimation as the musical comedies of today; it is only the passage of time which has given them classicality. The disintegration of comic opera in the nineteenth century seems to have begun about 1840, and it can be observed in Germany as well as in France; in both countries it is often difficult to draw the line between comic opera and operetta. Operetta never had much of a career in Italy; if there ever were any Italian

95

operettas they have passed completely into oblivion, and it is more likely that Italy drew upon the products of her neighbours for these things – that was at any rate the case during the period covered by the present writer's recollections. The sentimentalization of comic opera is a phenomenon which we have already observed in the eighteenth century, and its recurrence is probably due to the invariable desire of the general public to take all music seriously if it possibly can. The enjoyment of sentiment requires less intelligence than the appreciation of satire; and at the same time there is a large public which wants to hear great singers in trivial tunes.

It would be unjust to accuse Gounod of triviality; it is his sacred music rather than his operas which has won him the disapproval of those who uphold the canons of good taste. Of his religious sincerity there cannot be the least question, and if something of his ecclesiastical manner crept into *Faust*, it could hardly be said to be out of place in that environment. Another favourite opera of this period was *Mignon* (Paris, 1866) by Ambroise Thomas (1811–96), which enjoyed a lasting popularity in Germany, although the severer critics spoke of it as profanation of a great German classic (Goethe's novel, *Wilhelm Meister*).

A few years later came Bizet's *Carmen* (Paris, 1875), which enjoys undying popularity in all countries. *Carmen*, like *La Traviata*, is a historic landmark, for it was the first step towards naturalistic opera in the style which came to be called *verismo* in a later generation. It has many different claims on our admiration – a well constructed story, a picturesque environment happily translated into music by the use of Spanish melodies, although Spanish musicians often say there is nothing Spanish about the opera at all. *Carmen* is at any rate the classical source of what we may call 'operatic Spanish'. The music is an eternal delight, with its immediately attractive tunes and its ingenious and original turns of harmony and orchestration.

Saint-Saëns' (1835–1921) opera, *Samson and Delilah* (Weimar, 1877), was considered so modern and Wagnerian in its day that it had to wait many years before the Paris Opéra would accept it. It still holds the stage, but it is beginning to sound a little old-fashioned; that is the worst of what we might call

Bernardo Buontalenti, design for an Intermezzo, Florence, 1589.

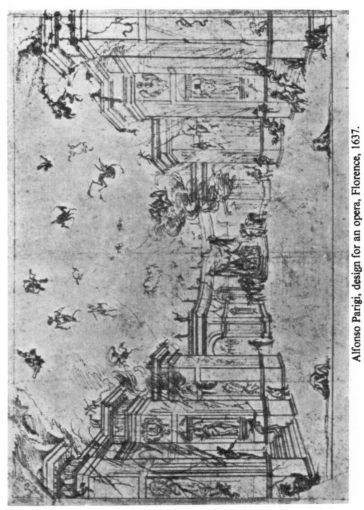

Alfonso Parigi, design for an opera, Florence, 1637.

Lodovico Burnacini, scene for *La Monarchia Latina Trionfante*, Vienna, 1678.

Lodovico Burnacini, scene for *La Monarchia Latina Trionfante*, Vienna, 1678.

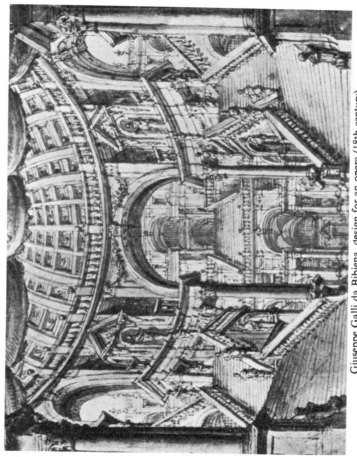

Giuseppe Galli da Bibiena, design for an opera (18th century).

James Thornhill, scene for *Arsinoe*, London, 1706.

C. F. Schinkel, scene for *The Magic Flute*, Berlin, 1816.

C. F. Schinkel, scene for *The Magic Flute*, Berlin, 1816.

Dandy fainting or — An Exquisite in Fits. Scene a Private Box
Opera

Isaac Robert Cruikshank, Dandies at the Opera, London, 1818.

(a) The Wolf's Glen in *Der Freischütz*, London, 1824.

(b) George Cruikshank, caricature of *Der Freischütz*, London, 1824.

Alessandro Sanquirico, scene for *Amleto* (Mercadante), Milan, 1822.

(a) *Lohengrin*, Weimar, 1850.

(b) *Rigoletto*, Venice, 1851.

Charles Reading, *Don Giovanni*, London, Sadler's Wells, 1938.

(a) Bagnall Harris, *Fidelio*, London, Sadler's Wells, 1937.

(b) Hans Strohbach, *Fra Diavolo*, London, Sadler's Wells, 1935.

Powell Lloyd, *Il Trovatore*, London, Sadler's Wells, 1939.

H. Procter-Gregg, *Hugh the Drover*, London, Sadler's Wells, 1937.

'the voluptuous school' – their charms are apt to fade with the passage of years. This is what has happened to some of the operas of Massenet (1842–1912), such as *Hérodiade* (Paris, 1881) and *Thaïs* (1894), in both of which the religious element was an added attraction. But *Manon* (1884) is an admirable example of Massenet's delicate sentimentality, and sentimentality is squeezed to the utmost drop in *Werther* (1886). Finally, in *Le Jongleur de Notre Dame* (1902), which combines sentiment with religion in a charmingly picturesque story, Massenet achieved his best work. To persons of robust tastes Massenet is unsympathetic, but it has to be admitted that his sentimentalities are executed with a craftsmanship of the very highest order.

The school of realism, the literary aspect of which was suggested mainly by the novels of Zola, was represented in France by Alfred Bruneau (1857–1934), who was a personal friend of Zola and wrote operas on librettos by him. Bruneau was followed by Charpentier (b. 1860), whose *Louise* (1900) has enjoyed considerable popularity. *Louise* was not a work of much originality; the music sounds rather like scraps of everything else and often has very little bearing on the play. But it was a work of great courage, for it put the slums of modern Paris on the stage with picturesque theatrical effect; and Charpentier's personal life has shown that its deep sense of human sympathy was absolutely genuine.

The landmark for *verismo* is Mascagni's (1863–1945) *Cavalleria Rusticana* (Rome, 1890), now inseparable from Leoncavallo's (1858–1919) *Pagliacci* (Milan, 1892), which was an obvious imitation of the former work. These two operas have become indispensable to every opera house in the world, but neither composer ever succeeded in producing another opera capable of holding the stage, although each made many attempts. Mascagni's later operas are revived from time to time, but none has become famous. For some reason or other there was a demand for operas in one act, and a large number of them were brought out in various countries; for an equally unknown reason the public seems now to have decided that it will not listen to one-act operas at all, apart from these two. The methods of *verismo* could, however, be equally well applied to full-length operas, and for some years stories of crime and low life were the favourite food of both composers and audiences. Here again we see a certain parallel to the movement which followed the French Revolution – with this difference, that whereas the sensational operas of the early nineteenth century made a point of a happy end and a high moral tone, those of the early twentieth preferred vicious characters and violent deaths.

Mascagni leads us naturally to his fellow-pupil Puccini (1858–1924), who by dint of far better musicianship and a very astute sense of the theatre in the choice of librettos secured himself more continuous popularity. His early opera, *Manon Lescaut* (Turin, 1893), has less charm than Massenet's treatment of the same story; with *La Bohème* (Turin, 1896) he achieved immediate success. Puccini was clever enough to learn from all his contemporaries. *La Bohème* combines the technique of *verismo* with the sentimentalism of Massenet in a far less restrained form. With Verdi heroic opera came to an end; *Falstaff* was heroic even though it was a comedy. Puccini frankly adopted the lower plane of *La Traviata* and every one of his operas exploits the woman who has loved too much. In *La Bohème* she is exactly the same type of Parisian dressmaker's apprentice that Charpentier presented in *Louise*; the difference of period is negligible, though in Puccini's case it was an excuse for picturesque costumes. For a hundred years Italian opera had made its appeal to the gallery, and in every gallery there must have been dozens of young women who could easily imagine themselves as Mimi. *Tosca* (Rome, 1900) was musically a great advance, though its story is repulsive; it was simply *verismo* in high life and period costume. Puccini's next opera, *Madame Butterfly*, was an ingenious mixture of modern dress and the picturesqueness of Japanese environment. It owes something to the English musical comedy, *The Geisha* (1892), which in those days was enormously popular in Italy. On its first production *Madame Butterfly* (Milan, 1904) was laughed off the stage, but it recovered very soon and is now almost more popular than *La Bohème*. The taste of the day was always for 'strong situations', and as Italian composers were beginning to realize the importance of America for the Italian opera trade Puccini chose an American subject for his next opera and had it brought out in New York – *The Girl of the Golden West* (1910), a work which has never attained the popularity of Puccini's previous operas. *La Rondine* (Monte Carlo, 1917) seems to have disappeared completely. Three one-act operas intended for a triple bill came out in Rome in 1919 – *Il Tabarro* (*The Cloak*), a lurid drama of low life in Paris, very effective on the stage, *Suor Angelica*, a sentimental tragedy in a nunnery with none but female characters, and a comic opera, *Gianni Schicchi*, which many people consider to be the best of all Puccini's works. The last of these was *Turandot* (Milan, 1926), based on Gozzi's fairy-tale of the eighteenth century; it was unfinished when Puccini died and was completed by Franco Alfano.

With Puccini's death another chapter of Italian operatic history comes to an end. Many new Italian operas have been produced in the last ten years, but not one of them appears to have secured a lasting success. *Turandot* marks the end of what one may call the general standard repertory; there remains to be considered in a later chapter a number of operas, some dating a good deal further back, which may be classed – at any rate for the present – as experimental.

There remain also to be noticed a few operas of a much older generation, which still command interest, although they stand somewhat outside the main lines of operatic history. One result of the Romantic Movement was to draw the attention of musicians to folk-music. *Der Freischütz*, with its popular German tunes, is the most conspicuous example of nationalist opera. In France and Italy folk-music was absorbed into romantic opera in a more unobtrusive way; it had been utilized so much in the early comic operas of the eighteenth century that there was no need to emphasize it in the nineteenth. But in other countries, where nationality itself stood in need of assertion, folk-music suddenly began to play an important part. Russia had hitherto contented itself with Italian opera, serious or comic, for the entertainment of the court and the nobility; in 1836 Glinka, an amateur of somewhat desultory musical education, produced *A Life for the Tsar*, a 'rescue opera' after the manner of Cherubini, but built mainly on types of melody which, if never actually Russian folk-songs, are conspicuously Russian in character. Poland achieved a similar 'national' opera in Moniuszko's *Halka* (1850), a work so little known outside its own country that its first German performance did not take place until 1934 at Hamburg. The most successful and the most widely known of all these folk-song operas of Slavonic Europe is Smetana's *The Bartered Bride* (1870); many other operas of Smetana are still popular in Prague.

Tchaikovsky (1840–93) hardly belongs to the 'nationalist' composers of Russia, but his *Eugene Oniegin* (1879) has an essentially Russian story from Pushkin as its foundation, and folk-music is introduced into it for the sake of local colour, not so much to emphasize nationality as to suggest the atmosphere of country life in contrast to that of the metropolis. Otherwise *Eugene Oniegin* is descended from *La Traviata*, and depends for its charm on a very sensitive delineation of character. A later opera, also on a story from Pushkin, *The Queen of Spades* (1890), has a more dramatic plot, though its music is less individual. The most intensely Russian of the Russian composers was Moussorgsky (1839–81), composer of *Boris Godunov* (1874) and *Khovanshchina,* left unfinished at the composer's death in 1881. These operas remained for many years almost unknown, and they did not begin to make their way in Western Europe until about 1910. They were a good deal retouched by Rimsky-Korsakov (1844–1908), and there has been considerable controversy over the relative merits of the various versions. The original version of *Boris Godunov* was recently staged at Sadler's Wells with great success, although it is more austere than the revision by Rimsky-Korsakov, which for a long time was the only accepted form of the opera. Both these operas are of the 'epic' type and deal with the history of Russia; they have too a definitely religious background which is hardly possible for a Western audience fully to appreciate. Rimsky-Korsakov left several operas which are effective on the stage, though all very much alike. They are mostly based on fantastic Russian legends; *Kitesh* (1907) has the characteristically Russian religious atmosphere. *The Snow Maiden* (1882) has had a lasting success at Sadler's Wells; *The Golden Cockerel*, his last opera (1909), based on a politico-satirical fairy-tale by Pushkin, is perhaps the best of all his works.

CHAPTER SEVEN

THE MUSICAL CONVENTIONS OF OPERA – RECITATIVE AND AIR – ENSEMBLES AND FINALES – POPULAR SONGS – CANONS – THE ORCHESTRA

HAVING reached the end of the usual repertory, we may now pause for a moment to consider in more detail the purely musical methods by which operas have been constructed. The first operas give us the first lists of what might be called orchestras. They are not unlike the lists of instruments in our own Jacobean masques; and it is obvious that the assemblage of a number of different instruments for the early operas must have been preceded many years before by similar assemblages for the innumerable spectacular entertainments of the small Italian courts. They made use of the usual system: either strings or wind, in families, with chord-playing instruments such as lutes and theorbos to fill up the harmony, assisted at need by the various types of spinet and virginal, and also by small chamber organs. It was not the custom in those days to print or even to write out full scores in the modern way. The earliest operas of Peri, Caccini and Monteverdi were printed probably at the expense of some prince, for private distribution as souvenirs, like our own masques, for as in the masques the stage directions are all given in the past tense, a record of a thing that had happened, not a direction for future performance. The notable exception is Cavalieri's *Anima e Corpo*, the printed score of which was clearly intended for future performances; but as this is a strictly religious work it would be performed under very different conditions. In the operas, lists of instruments are given, but the only music printed is the voice part and a figured bass; it is obvious that this is no more than a skeleton outline of the score, and various theories have been advanced as to what the instruments played. Some people have supposed that they all improvised their parts from the figured bass; it seems much more likely that they

101

had manuscript parts to play from and that these were lost after the performance. Monteverdi's *Orfeo* tells us more, but not enough; there are various parts for instruments printed here and there, mostly of a rather startling character. A study of later operas leads one to imagine that most of the declamation was accompanied by lutes, harpsichord or organ alone, the choice being sometimes indicated. It is clear that in these days there was no regular school of operatic singing, for the simple reason that opera was a novelty; and it is also clear that what the promoters aimed at more than anything else was the declamation of the words. If there was anything like a complicated orchestral accompaniment, the words would not be heard. This practice was continued for over a hundred years; even at the beginning of the eighteenth century the general principle is to accompany the voice lightly and let the noisier instruments come in when it has finished. It was just at that time, about 1700, as we can see from the scores of Alessandro Scarlatti, that the question arose – which are the noisy instruments? Before 1700, more or less, the noisy ones that must be kept in the background are the violins; after 1700 string-playing has improved so much that they can now be trusted with the delicate task of accompanying a singer; and harpsichords have grown so big that they are more usefully employed to give fullness to the *tutti* after the voice has ended. And by that time, too, opera has got well under way and opera singing has become a regular profession.

The first step towards making these early music-dramas more musical was to break up the monotony of the declamation with lyrical refrains, and gradually these refrains expanded into regular songs. As soon as opera became an established form of entertainment there was more and more demand for clearly defined songs, and this demand naturally became all the more insistent after 1637 when opera at Venice was thrown open to the public on payment. It was a short step from songs to duets. And the more the interest of the audience became concentrated on the songs, the quicker the intervening dialogue had to be got through, so that in place of the tedious declamation of rather precious and affected poetry we get rapid conversation, sometimes on very commonplace matters. That has always been the eternal problem of opera – how to

102

manage the plain statements about commonplace things which are unavoidable in order to keep the drama going. The Italians solved it quite early in the seventeenth century by a stereotyped form of recitative which continued into the nineteenth. It was called *recitativo secco* ('dry recitative') and was accompanied merely by a bass-viol holding the bass in slow notes, and a harpsichord filling up the minimum of harmony. If we look at it from our end of history, it may well seem absurd; it is music reduced to such a minimum that surely it would be simpler to do without music altogether and revert to plain speech. But it is clear that it was derived from the original declamation of the first operas, and that declamation was the very *raison d'être* of the whole operatic idea. Much depends on whether the words declaimed are metrical or not, and whether one can conveniently beat time to their musical setting. In the earliest operas this is the general rule; melody is reduced to the melody of speech, but rhythm is never absent. Later, when recitative became more naturalistic, the verse became free, and regular metrical rhythm disappeared; it is at this point that recitative seems to cease to be music. It continued to exist in this hybrid style, because it was easier to keep up an established tradition than to break with it altogether.

It was a long time before people began to resent recitative in any country. Each language outside Italy very soon found the musical idiom that was best suited to it; what was resented in later days was either recitative in a foreign language which nobody understood, or Italian recitative translated into a language to which inflexions were not appropriate. At the beginning of the eighteenth century recitative was sometimes accompanied by the stringed instruments; this was only possible when violins had learned to play with some refinement, and it was used only for specially dramatic moments, moments of deep emotion. Many readers will remember that in Bach's *St Matthew Passion* the Evangelist is supported only by the harpsichord or organ, and so are all the other characters in the story except Jesus. His utterances are always accompanied by the strings, the sound of which gives these sacred words a certain mystery; it ought to be remembered that when Handel introduces the strings in a recitative, sacred or secular, he does it for the same sort of purpose, to shift the dialogue on to a higher plane of emotion. In later years composers wanted to keep the whole of the dialogue at this emotional level, and did away with 'dry' recitative altogether; the result was that their accompanied recitative is often more dry than it would have been otherwise.

It is easy for us who have been brought up on Wagner and modern orchestral concerts to be scornful about the opera of Handel's time as being nothing more than a concert in costume. A concert in costume had some justification in those days, when concerts, such as we have now, scarcely existed. When Dr Johnson – who by the way was confessedly quite unmusical – called opera 'an exotick and irrational entertainment' it was the *Italian* opera in London that he was attacking; the context shows that he had no objection to English opera (Life of John Hughes, in *Lives of the Poets*). Exotic and irrational it was, and why not? Since the days of ancient Rome people have always enjoyed the exotic, something foreign and strange, and it might quite well be argued that it was the business of music, and indeed of all art, to be irrational. Opera was certainly irrational enough in the Venice of the seventeenth century. Venice in those days was the chief pleasure city of Europe, and was visited, especially during the carnival, by enormous numbers of foreigners. As the climate of Venice is at its very worst from Christmas to Easter, it is obvious that indoor amusements must have constituted the chief attraction. But a journey to Venice was an expensive undertaking in those days, and the foreign visitors were mostly German princes and other wealthy people. The *Mercure Galant*, a periodical published in Paris, gives many accounts of the Venetian operas, but it is noteworthy that they are described almost exclusively as shows for the eye. It was a long time before the promoters of operas knew what they really wanted; but it became clear at a very early stage that nobody wanted the rather dreary and academic entertainments of Peri and Caccini. Commercial opera at Venice at once standardized operatic methods of all kinds; the heterogeneous orchestra of Monteverdi was reduced to something like a classical orchestra, based on the string quartet and pairs of wind instruments. Songs and dances were freely introduced, and one result of this was the interplay of voice and instruments in the course of a song. This alternation of singing and playing, phrases first sung by a voice and then echoed by the violins, which is so familiar to us in the songs of Handel, was a gradual development. How far it was connected with dancing is not very clear, but the stage directions in some of the old Venetian operas show plainly that gestures and movements were often timed to music.

Dance music in the older Italian operas always seems to be rather primitive, but although the French were generally considered to be the leaders in the art of dancing in the seventeenth century, certain forms are to be found almost universally. It has never yet been finally settled whether the lilting rhythm that is most familiar to English people as 'Hush-a-bye, baby, on the tree top' came from these islands, or from France, or from the Friuli, the country north of Venice, from which the name *Forlana* was given to a dance in that rhythm. In Handel's day it came to be called *Siciliana*, and in the days of Mendelssohn it was supposed to be the rhythm of the *Barcarola*, the supposed song of Venetian gondoliers; but it is not characteristic of the Venetian boat songs in the eighteenth century.

The 'good taste' of Zeno and Metastasio, which reduced Handelian opera to the formula of the concert in costume, had at any rate one good result; it permitted the greater development of the single song, and the dramatic use of florid singing. This was soon abused, and another reform had to come in the days of Gluck. It is curious that one of the worst faults of the great Wagnerian operas is the weariness resulting from so much solo singing, which was exactly the fault of the opera before Gluck came on the scene. As with Wagner, so with Handel (I use the name of Handel to stand for all his generation), it was not good operatic manners for one singer to interrupt another (except in recitative) or to carry on any sort of discussion in music. Fortunately, the comic operas were not hampered by this rule of behaviour. They were intended to be lifelike and amusing, and composers very soon saw that they could make a good effect by setting two people to quarrel and call each other names in a duet. As this sort of thing generally came towards the end of an act, the device was expanded into a 'concerted finale' as it came to be called, in which several characters came on the stage and engaged in conversation that took the form of a regular piece of music. There was another sort of ensemble, which it is convenient to call the 'ensemble of perplexity', placed not at the end of an act, but somewhere in the middle, at a moment when several characters are faced with a difficult situation. This was invented by Alessandro Scarlatti and first used by him in a comic opera (1718); he liked the idea so much that he used it first in a perfectly serious situation, shaping it like an ordinary air, only divided between four characters, and then later on caricatured it by writing another quartet in the same opera for four comic characters whose conversation is more life-like than melodious.

In the course of the century the comic-finale was much extended. At first it was rather inclined to tail off at the end because in those days no curtain fell until the very end of the opera, which meant that the characters had to be got off the stage somehow, and generally the chief comedian was left to the last in the character of an angry old man. By the time we reach Mozart it is evident that each act ended with a curtain, for the finales are now built up so as to begin quietly with one or two characters, and bring on more, one after another, so as to end with six or seven people all singing together like a chorus. Mozart's librettist, Da Ponte, tells us in his memoirs how difficult it was to write words for scenes of this kind; as a matter of fact he was as skilful as anybody in building up finales. Another use of the ensemble was to start the opera; and it has been pointed out how several of Goldoni's plays begin with a scene for several characters all in a group on the stage when the curtain rises, just as if they were to sing a sextet – the idea was certainly derived from comic opera.

The chorus took little part in these operas, serious or comic. The old Venetian operas employed large quantities of supers; whenever a king or queen came on they were always accompanied by a huge train of attendants. But these people had little or nothing to sing, as they were not intelligent enough to learn complicated music. The chorus was treated more seriously in France, and that is why we do occasionally find both chorus and ballet in the London operas of Handel, for though they are Italian in language they sometimes took over the methods of Paris. The comic operas at Naples and Venice were much humbler and cheaper entertainments, and no doubt the

106

reason why they had no chorus was simply that they could not afford it.

There is one feature of the Neapolitan comic operas which must be mentioned here, because it started a tradition that lasted well into the nineteenth century; that was the *canzonetta*, a popular song of folk-song type, generally in the local dialect, and sung by some very humble character. The Neapolitan songs were generally in six-eight time, and sometimes in old modes, like some of our own folk-songs. This type of song passed into the French comic operas, too, with certain local modifications, and in the French operas it nearly always took the form of a ballad with several verses, the function of which was to tell the audience some story that was essential to the drama. Mozart's *Figaro* and *Don Giovanni* show the Italian *canzonetta* still surviving in Susanna's song, 'Deh vieni, non tardar', and in Don Giovanni's serenade, 'Deh vieni alla finestra'. We see it again in Zerlina's ballad in *Fra Diavolo* and in Senta's ballad in *The Flying Dutchman*; in both these cases it is the French type of narrative song.

Verdi said in a letter that he wanted to make *Rigoletto* a series of duets, and Mozart might have said much the same thing about *Figaro*. Verdi's letter was provoked by the request of a lady that Gilda might be given another song to herself; Mozart found himself in trouble at the end of *Figaro* because he had written too many duets, and the singers all claimed their solo airs as a matter of right, so that the last act of *Figaro* is cumbered with several airs that are now nearly always omitted in performance. Mozart and the composers of his time were faced with a new problem. Music in general was moving towards the symphony as the standard type of large work, and one can see that Mozart was gradually tending to make his operas more and more continuous. In *Figaro* it is no great loss to substitute spoken dialogue for the *secco* recitatives, as was always done in Germany until the present century; in *Don Giovanni* it is a fact that the same practice held good in Germany in many theatres, but in English we feel it regrettable. In *Così fan Tutte* it is indispensable to sing the recitatives, because they often glide insensibly into the set pieces. *The Magic Flute* starts as a German comic opera with a good deal of spoken dialogue, but as the play proceeds the dialogue becomes less and less, and the 'finale' of the second act – so called because it is all continuous music – covers several separate scenes. The difficulty was to find a way of carrying on the story without breaking up the music, and that was a purely technical problem of musical composition.

Musicians have always wanted to achieve some sort of musical drama which should be all air without any recitative; one might as well try to make a sandwich that should be all jam without any bread. There was a very early attempt in France at an opera of this kind, but it must have been nothing more than a refinement and elaboration of the old English 'jigs' in which a whole play was acted sung to a ballad tune. The French generally took the view that music was a decoration superimposed on the play, and that the play had to explain itself independently of the music.

Mozart gets a little way towards solving the problem in his finales, and he had also the accompanied recitative at his disposal; but really the accompanied recitative was not so very much more musical than the *secco*. The real test is whether one can beat time to it. Purcell had found his own solution in *Dido and Aeneas*, where the dialogue is all in rhymed verse and set to music which hovers between singing and declamation, as the composer thinks appropriate, but always in unbroken musical rhythm, so that one can beat time to it all the way through. But *Dido and Aeneas* is a miniature, and it may be doubted whether the method could have been carried out on a larger scale. Gluck has always been held up to admiration for having abolished the harpsichord in the opera – that is, for making all his recitatives accompanied by the orchestra. In performance these recitatives are often dreary, and the same thing can be said of the French composers who followed him, such as Spontini and Lesueur. But the French did gradually make a little progress with getting more of the story told in the course of musical numbers, for the French always laid great stress on the conversational style of setting words to music. The Italians preferred attractive melody and obvious vocal effects, and when one compares contemporaries, as, for instance, Dalayrac and Paer setting the same libretto of *Camilla*, the Italian seems professional and the Frenchman almost an amateur.

108

A device which is characteristic of this period – i.e., about 1800 – is the canon or round. The first example of its employment in opera seems to be in the second act of *Così fan Tutte*, where Mozart brings it in very appropriately and indeed naturally. The two couples are having supper together to celebrate their engagements, which, as we know, are fictitious. The supper-party has reached a rather rapturous stage, and one of the ladies proposes to drink a health. This is taken up in canon by the second lady and the tenor. Canons of this kind were popular in Italy and in Vienna, too; Mozart's old teacher, Padre Martini, wrote quantities of them, many very melodious and attractive. Like Purcell's catches, they were things to sing on convivial occasions. But on this particular occasion the bass, who should have been the fourth voice, refuses to join in. The plain fact is that he cannot, because the tune is too high for him; so Mozart with his invariable ingenuity and happy sense of the stage, makes him get up from the table and give vent to his private feelings of indignation. Paer and Cherubini were the next people to seize on this idea of singing a round in an opera; but they use it more as an 'ensemble of perplexity', or sometimes of unanimity, quite apart from convivial surroundings and simply as a musical form. The next, and the best-known example, is the canon in *Fidelio*, very much an 'ensemble of perplexity'; one sometimes finds this movement spoken of as if it was a piece of elaborate academic ingenuity, which is nonsense. The effect of it on the stage is quite different from that produced by Mozart; Mozart makes it a piece of realism and activity, for as each successive voice enters with the tune, the alcoholic atmosphere becomes thicker and Guglielmo's bad temper takes the situation a stage further. Beethoven's quartet, on the other hand, is deeply serious, though the situation on the stage is quite static. Nothing happens; the four people must take up their positions and poses and hold them from beginning to end. They cannot move, and that is the real difficulty of this quartet – to sing it in such a way that the intensity of feeling set by the instrumental introduction is never let down. That quiet prelude for the lower strings only is the moment when Beethoven first hints to us that this play is going to be something more than a pretty little comedy; Beethoven is about the first composer to discover how to express, instrumentally, the *suppression* of an intense emotion.

The complex finale was generally kept for the second act of an opera; it obviously could not be repeated in all three, and generally the third act, after the pages of recitative that at last untied all the tangle of misrepresentation on which the plot was constructed, had become rather long and required a quick conclusion. A favourite method was the French *vaudeville* in which each character came forward and sang a little verse in turn to the same tune, the rest joining in a chorus. Gluck's *Orpheus* ends like this, and so does *Idomeneo*; in courtly 'tragedy', which always had to have a happy end, the vaudeville was like the *licenza* of old Italian plays, a formal taking leave of the audience after the play was over. The same form serves for the end of *The Seraglio*, and we find it again at the end of *The Barber of Seville*.

The persistence of musical forms which have no dramatic reason for their existence is very curious; the fact is that when opera becomes commercialized, every composer imitates something that he thinks successful. It was probably the partition of Poland which made the *polonaise* or *polacca* fashionable towards the end of the eighteenth century. Cherubini's *Lodoiska* is on a Polish subject, and it was appropriate that the comic servant should sing a polonaise in the first act, and equally appropriate for a girl to dance one in his second Polish opera, *Faniska* (1806). But just the same sort of polonaise occurs in Gaveaux's *Léonore* (1798), the first version of the *Fidelio* story, although here it is evidently intended to sound Spanish. Beethoven wrote polacca movements; Schubert and Weber both wrote polonaises, and the type went on and on through the romantic movement – Ännchen sings one in *Der Freischütz* – until the days of Verdi and Ambroise Thomas ('Je suis Titania' in *Mignon*).

The reappearance of the chorus in opera has already been mentioned in a previous chapter. At a period when ensembles were becoming more and more symphonic, the chorus was very useful as adding to the total noise. A conspicuous example of an over-noisy ensemble is that in the first scene of *The Barber of Seville*. Count Almaviva has hired musicians to serenade Rosina; as the serenade has to come to an abrupt

110

end, he dismisses them. A very amusing effect is then made by the exaggerated gratitude of the musicians on receiving their fees, and the annoyance of the Count at the noise they are making and the difficulty of getting rid of them. This exploitation of nuisance-value is certainly a very characteristic picture of Italian life, and might have happened any day in Naples, and probably in Seville, too. But Rossini carries the joke too far and carries it on too long and too noisily. The ensembles of Mozart's comic operas seldom employed the chorus at all, but he made an advance in stage technique when he built up choral finales in *La Clemenza di Tito* which are designed quite differently from both the conventional comic finale and the *vaudeville* of Gluck.

A notable feature of the first finale in *La Clemenza di Tito*, which represents Rome being set on fire, is that it ends softly. The dramatic point of the scene is not the pictorial effect of the fire, but the horror of everybody at the crime of arson. The *diminuendo* finale was taken up by some of the French composers of the Revolution period, though it is hardly likely that they got the idea so quickly from Mozart; but it was not a device that appealed to Italians, and a German critic recorded in the 1820s that Mozart's operas made no effect on Italian audiences because so many of the numbers ended softly. That meant, of course, that the Italian audience was taken by surprise and missed its chances of applauding.

The later French operas, and all those of Rossini, were well guarded against dangers of this kind, for they developed their finales on a gigantic scale. It was the period of enormous opera houses, especially in Italy, where many new ones were built; and it is the period of all those absurd conventions which have made opera the laughing-stock of serious music-lovers. If one sees a skit on opera in an entertainment of the *Chauve-souris* type one may be sure that it will make fun of the opera as it was in the days of Donizetti. In France people went mainly to see the spectacle, in Italy and in London to listen to singers.

The main contribution of Germany was the development of the orchestra. It has been said by a German critic that the orchestra of the romantic theatre represented all those super-natural powers against which mortal man was vainly struggling. It certainly was used to represent the forces of nature which played so important a part in the early romantic operas of Hoffmann and Weber. At the same time it is necessary to point out that the Germans were not the first inventors of 'atmospheric' music of this kind. The classical examples of storms in music are those in Haydn's *Seasons* (1801) and Beethoven's *Pastoral Symphony* (1808); but Paer's *Camilla* (1801) and Méhul's *Uthal* (1805) both begins with preludes depicting storms.

The most important contribution of Wagner to the purely musical technique of opera was the *leitmotiv* or guiding theme. Characters, places, events, states of mind, anything in fact that enters into the drama, can be associated with some definite musical theme, and this theme is woven into the orchestral texture whenever Wagner wishes to remind us of the thing represented. Sometimes the themes are pictorially representative, but in the majority of cases they are not, though they are always musically expressive and interesting. German commentators naturally expended much energy in listing these themes, and in discovering new ones, for not every single one was pointed out by Wagner himself. In a vast work like *The Ring* the guiding themes fulfil two functions – they give us information about the drama, telling us sometimes what is passing in the unspoken thoughts of a character, and they also give musical unity to the whole work, like the themes of a Beethoven's symphony.

They are closely connected, too, with Wagner's abolition of the chorus and his statement that he wished the orchestra to take the place of the chorus – that is, of the chorus in Greek tragedy, which commented on the action of the drama from time to time. Wagner's orchestra is, however, not a series of interludes, such as the Greek chorus supplied, but an unbroken commentary. It thus ceases to be a support and accompaniment to the voices; it becomes the voice of Wagner himself perpetually talking, talking, talking, so much so that people are often quite content to listen to orchestral excerpts from Wagner without the voices which ought to be dominating them.

This view of the orchestra easily led Wagner on to the enlargement of its forces. Spontini had set the bad example long before, but Wagner carried his extravagance still further and made a principle of demanding three of each wind instrument where there had formerly been two in order that complete chords might be played in one and the same quality of tone. More wind needed more strings; besides, Wagner very often liked to divide the strings into many parts. The brass was largely increased in every department, and singers naturally complained that their voices would be destroyed if they attempted to sing against such huge volumes of sound. It was for this reason that Wagner constructed the sunken orchestra at Bayreuth, in which the different sounds of the instruments are blended and mellowed. Wagner's orchestration has often been compared to the 'full swell' of a large organ, so that it is very appropriate to the transmitting mechanism of the gramophone and the wireless which make all orchestras sound more or less like a harmonium.

The large orchestra needed large voices to cope with it, and the last half century or so has seen the emergence of the specific Wagner singer, male and female. In the eighteenth century the tenor was the voice for old men (and for old women, too, very often); when the *castrati* went out of fashion there appeared the *tenore di grazia*, trained on their methods, and the ideal interpreter of Bellini. It was not until Verdi's days that the *tenore di forza* came into prominence, and Wagner's heroic parts could only be sung adequately by a new type, the *Heldentenor*, who is generally a forced-up baritone.

Wagner, like all romantics, wanted to do away with recitative and, indeed, with *aria* as well; he professed to have created a system of 'endless *melos*' – using the Greek word for the sake of dignity, because in his mind 'melody' had acquired a bad reputation. Nobody would say nowadays that there was no melody in Wagner, though that was the favourite accusation brought against him in his own time. But the Wagnerian melody has its drawbacks; in order to give the singers a chance against the orchestra, Wagner makes them all sing very slowly, in long-drawn-out notes. The German language permits this; English rebels against it. Even in German it is always difficult to hear the words in a Wagner opera, though Wagner himself wanted them to be on a level with the music.

And this prolongation of notes means that all the singers often appear to be singing *adagio* even when the orchestra, expressing the real mood of the drama, is going at a brisk speed. Perhaps it all helps to suggest the 'heroic' stature of Wagner's characters, but it also accounts for the fact that some of them tend to become bores, notably Wolfram in *Tannhäuser* and that worst bore of all opera, Gurnemanz in *Parsifal*.

In *The Mastersingers* Wagner reverted to a more traditional technique. The chorus is used just as it was in *Das Liebesverbot,* except that it now has very much more difficult music to sing, and there is plenty of ensemble writing, including the famous quintet, which is always the most popular number of the opera. In the second act we observe a new and ingenious, if somewhat risky device, adopted by Verdi, too, in the third act of *Otello;* the finale is built up to a great *fortissimo* and then suddenly broken off, leaving the stage to a single character on whom the curtain falls. In both these cases the result is highly successful, though the effects desired are dramatically very different. Wagner's scene is a street brawl, interrupted by the blast of the watchman's horn which frightens everybody back into their houses. Their exits take a little time, and several bars of instrumental music have to cover this, making a general *diminuendo*; then the watchman comes in to call the hour, and after he has gone out the stage remains empty in the moonlight for quite a long time while Wagner goes on thinking about the situation in the orchestra. The whole scene is a masterly piece of stagecraft and musically fascinating as well; but what holds our attention breathless is the orchestra and what Wagner himself has to say to us.

Contrast this with Verdi's method in *Otello*. Othello has just gone through a fearful scene with Iago, who works him up to the last agonies of jealousy against Desdemona; at that moment trumpets are heard announcing the arrival of the Venetian ambassadors. Othello must receive them and go through with the ceremony. The stage fills with people and the music is gradually built up to great masses of sound. In the middle of the ceremony Othello loses control of himself and accuses Desdemona in public; this is just the situation for a great ensemble, as in *Trovatore* (end of Act II) and in *Traviata* (end of Act III). But instead of the ensemble ending with the conventional *fortissimo* of everybody, it is broken off; Othello turns everybody out, and then collapses unconscious, and the act ends with the triumph of Iago while distant trumpets and a cheering chorus are heard as an ironical comment on the situation. There is a curious resemblance between the two operas which may or may not be accidental – the distant trumpets in Verdi, and the orchestral reminiscence of the brawling motive in Wagner; but there is a fundamental difference – Wagner wants the stage for himself, Verdi gives it to the actual character who at this moment is dominating the drama.

Verdi did not want to give up any of the old musical devices; he only gave up the devices for catching applause in the wrong place. If *Rigoletto* was to be a succession of duets, *Falstaff* comes very near being a continuous ensemble; but it is always an ensemble of voices, and a conductor who ignores the voices will ruin the opera. Verdi did not trouble his head about guiding themes; he used characteristic themes and developed them as he happened to want them, but without anything of the dogmatic system of Wagner. And as one might expect, the use of recurrent themes was not Wagner's own invention; we find it in *Idomeneo*, and (in an almost Wagnerian way) in Méhul's *Ariodant* (1799).

The *veristi* did not bother much about technique or musical construction; they went straight for violence of contrast and the most obvious effects of vocal expression. It was they who bred – and Puccini who utilized – the typical products of the modern Italian opera stage, the wobbling soprano who is never on her true note, and the gulping tenor always on the verge of collapsing into tears. We must in justice admire Puccini's masterly skill in the handling of all his resources, voices, stage situations and orchestra, but there is something repellent about the huge financial business that Puccini's operas have become. It is not merely the actual performances of the operas in Italy and all over the world, but the sending out of Italian companies to sing them abroad, the wireless and gramophone royalties, and those collected from every hotel and restaurant band that plays its daily selection from *Bohème* and *Butterfly*. The profits must be gigantic, and equally gigantic, therefore, was the risk that attended every first night of a new opera at the Scala or the Costanzi. Puccini was a clever man of business; his operas had to be up to date, with all the post-Wagnerian technique, but at the same time they had to be all divisible into sections that would each make a gramophone record.

CHAPTER EIGHT

LIBRETTOS – SCENERY – ACTING

IT is generally imagined that all opera librettos are nonsense and doggerel. This is not the case, for in the first operas the words were probably considered much more important than the music. The dramas which Rinuccini wrote for musical setting were highly literary, one might almost say precious. They were intended to reproduce the spirit of Greek tragedy; they were not intended to surprise the audience. Everybody knew the story; what they expected was to hear beautiful poetry spoken to musical notes and to admire beautiful dresses and scenery. Those audiences knew what poetry was; they had heard Greek plays acted in Italian, and they all knew such plays as Guarini's *Pastor Fido* and Tasso's *Aminta*, one of the loveliest poems ever written.

The libretto of the first opera, *Dafne*, by Ottavio Rinuccini, has been preserved, but the music is lost except for two small fragments. It begins with a prologue sung by the poet Ovid, who explains who he is and salutes the illustrious company present. The first scene is laid in a forest where a chorus of nymphs and shepherds are in great fear of the Python. Apollo appears, after a chorus in which he answers their questions in the manner of an echo; they beg him to slay the monster and he does so. After a solo in which he reassures them, they sing a song of acclamation, and ask what tree has leaves worthy to wreathe his head.

The next scene brings on Venus and Cupid; Apollo meets them and teases Cupid about his bow and arrows, asking if he is hunting serpents, too. Cupid is much annoyed and challenges Apollo to a duel. The chorus sing an interlude about Cupid and his arrows. Daphne enters as a huntress and meets Apollo, who makes love to her; she refuses his advances, flies and is pursued by him. Re-enter Venus and Cupid; Cupid claims a great triumph because he has made Apollo fall in love. After another choral song a shepherd enters and tells the chorus how Daphne was turned into a laurel tree. Apollo enters and after a song of lamentation he takes his lyre and sings a song of praise to the laurel that is to make crowns for kings and poets. Another chorus brings the opera to an end.

Few directions are given for the stage; we are told that Apollo must take care to strike the serpent exactly on the right word of the chorus, and that the serpent must be very big and terrifying. It was to move its wings and spout fire; 'soppra tutto serpeggi', above all it must wriggle, and the man who worked it from inside must go on all fours. The chorus were to be not less than sixteen or eighteen singers, and were generally to stand in a half-moon formation. They are to move to the right and the left during their song of triumph (the serpent is to run away after being wounded), but they are to avoid anything like dancing. Since it is very difficult for a singer to make a good show of slaying the serpent, which is more a dancer's business, and since all this leaping about might tire him too much, it is suggested that two people should be dressed as Apollo, exactly alike, one to do the killing, and the other to come out and take his place to sing the song; we are told that this was actually done at every performance and that nobody was any the wiser. Another useful hint to the actor is that when Apollo sings his final song about the laurel, he must have a sprig of laurel in his hand and wreathe his own head with it. This is rather difficult; the sprig must not be too big, nor too small, and the way to manage it is to have two sprigs of the same length, fastened together by the tips. Apollo must hold these in his hand together, so that they look like one sprig; then at the right moment he divides them as he puts them to his head, and as they are joined in front all he has to do is to tie the ribbons together at the back.

Yet another useful direction: when Apollo sings his last song he must take his lyre and play. The 'lyre' must have been a viol with a bow, such as Apollo plays in Raphael's fresco, for four real players are to stand hidden in the wings and play in harmony, taking care to bow exactly together so that it sounds as if Apollo was playing it all himself. 'This deception cannot be detected by anyone who is not in the secret and it always gives no little delight.'

Euridice (1600), also by Rinuccini, was a slightly more elaborate affair as regards scenery, as far as can be ascertained. The poem is about the same length as *Dafne*, and, like that opera, it consists of short scenes separated by choruses. Orpheus and Eurydice are about to be married; first we see Eurydice with her friends, and then Orpheus with his – love has made him rather melancholy. Daphne, a nymph, comes on and hesitatingly breaks the news of Eurydice's death. Orpheus, after a most moving recitative, leaves the stage; the chorus sing a lament. In the next scene Arcetro, a shepherd, gives a long account of how he saw Orpheus grieving in despair alone, and how Venus came down from heaven to console him. The scene now changes from a wood to the mouth of Hades. Venus brings in Orpheus and tells him to proceed and try to move Pluto with his song. The rocks divide and show the burning city of Dis. Orpheus sings to Pluto, who allows himself to be persuaded by Proserpine, though Rhadamanthus and Charon try to hold him firm; Pluto gives way and allows Orpheus to take Eurydice back to earth without imposing any conditions. The wood scene returns, and Amyntas, another shepherd, tells the astonished chorus that he has seen Orpheus and Eurydice together. Finally the happy pair enter and the opera concludes with a chorus.

Note that Orpheus does not lose Eurydice again, as he does in the legend; and notice also the curious way in which no less than three events are described by messengers. It is interesting to compare this *Orfeo* with the *Orfeo* of Monteverdi, for which a different libretto was written by Alessandro Striggio. This from a dramatic point of view is much stronger than Rinuccini's play, which to the modern reader is too formal and precious in style. Striggio, after a prologue sung by a figure representing Music, starts at once with the wedding of Orpheus and Eurydice, though Eurydice does not appear. Much stress is laid on the contrast between the joy which Orpheus is now feeling and the sufferings which he had to endure before. In the second act the nymph Silvia announces the death of Eurydice from the bite of a serpent. The chorus condoles with Orpheus. Here the scene changes. The third act shows us Orpheus at the gate of Hades, accompanied by Hope, who says she must now leave him, quoting the well-known line of Dante – 'Abandon hope, all ye who enter here.' Orpheus meets Charon, who, as usual, is a slightly humorous figure; he sends Charon to sleep with his song and then steps into his boat, which takes him across the Styx; the act ends with a chorus of infernal spirits. Act IV opens with Proserpine begging Pluto to allow Orpheus to take back Eurydice; Pluto agrees, on condition that Orpheus is not to look at her until they have left Hades. He orders that *both* of them – this is made very clear – are to be informed of this condition. After a short chorus there is a pleasing little episode in which Proserpine and Pluto show their affection for one another. Orpheus enters, singing rather exuberantly of the triumph that his lyre has won; he cares nothing for the condition imposed by Pluto and insists that love has a higher claim. He looks at Eurydice, and a noise is heard behind the scenes. He sees Eurydice die, and a solitary spirit voice tells him that he has broken the law and is unworthy of grace. Eurydice, after a short lament, is taken back by spirits; the chorus sing a little ode on the virtue of self-control. In Act V Orpheus is in the fields of Thrace, where after a dialogue with an echo he vows that he will never love woman again. At this point the printed libretto diverges entirely from the printed score. In the libretto Orpheus sees a troop of Bacchantes coming and at once flies from them in horror, after which there is a long chorus in praise of Bacchus; Monteverdi must have seen that this made a very unsatisfactory end, so he makes Apollo come down in a cloud and take Orpheus up to heaven. Apollo's cloud

120

must have been admired, for it was evidently kept for another occasion, and in 1608 he came down in it again to sing the prologue to *Arianna*.

This second version of the Orpheus legend is not only better laid out, but is much more forcible in its language, the whole emotional atmosphere is intensified. The poem is still on a high literary level; it was taken for granted that the audience would consist entirely of persons of classical culture.

These early operas do not seem to have required very much in the way of elaborate scenery; the later extravagances of decoration started at Rome, where Cardinal Barberini gave marvellous performances in his own palace. His private theatre could hold four thousand spectators. In the history of stage machinery opera holds a more important place than drama; all the inventions of the stage engineers and architects in the seventeenth century were intended for operas. Many designs for stage scenes were engraved, but very naturally the engravers drew what the architect wanted the scene to look like, and not what one would have seen in reality. The general principle of construction is always that of a series of wings, either parallel to the line of the footlights, or pointing slightly towards the back. At the back there was a back-cloth painted in deceptive perspective. The great majority of scenes are architectural; even when the stage represents a garden, it consists mainly of colonnades or other architectural decorations. Even a scene consisting entirely of trees would be made in the same way, each wing ingeniously suggesting a walk down an alley of cypresses or poplars. Some of the scenes appear to be constructed on the arch principle, each pair of wings, right and left, being continued across the top without a break; this was useful for scenes representing caves. But it is probable that the engraver has concealed the joins with the curved sky-borders, for in those days prosceniums were enormously high, and it was not until about the beginning of the nineteenth century that back-cloths and cut-cloths could be taken up into the flies; back-cloths were always rolled for want of space above.

The engravings often leave the sky completely free, as if the theatres had cycloramas in the most modern style. This gives a curious absurdity to the wings, for the columns stand in rows with nothing for them to support. What we now call box-scenes were quite unknown; even in interiors where there are borders above representing beams the wings still remain parallel with the footlights. They could not be set any other way, for they moved in grooves or slots, either towards the stage or away from it. Each wing was connected with a winch under the stage, where at a given signal the scene-shifters could cause every wing (generally six on each side) to disappear simultaneously, leaving another set of wings visible just behind the first set.

When the public operas were established at Venice, the expenses of scenery had to be more carefully considered, although eventually a few of the Venetian theatres were subsidized by the noble families to whom they belonged. The designs that were engraved were naturally only those for the more magnificent occasions. French travellers gave wonderful accounts of the marvels of the Venetian stage, with live elephants and camels as well as horses; but other critics, less credulous, tell us that the animals were artificial and very skilfully made. We read of Orpheus singing on the stage to an audience of beasts both wild and tame, with trees that bowed in true Shakespearean fashion; and the most extraordinary sight must have been the artificial monkey which 'climbed on the back of other animals, picked fleas off their heads and did all sorts of other things just like a real monkey'. The allegorical operas performed at Vienna went in for elaborate symbolism, as for instance when the four elements were represented by a lion, a fiery dragon, a sea-monster and a peacock, who performed a sort of dance together. In one of the Venetian operas an act ends with horses being sacrificed to Mars; 'proud of having been elected to so high an honour, they express their delight in a curious (*bizarro*) dance'.

Monteverdi stood out against the decadence of the opera, although in his last opera, *The Coronation of Poppaea* (1642), he yielded to the new taste for melodious airs in preference to perpetual recitative. The words were by Francesco Busenello, who had a fine sense of the stage and a dignified literary style. Monteverdi in his letters shows himself to have shared the determination of Verdi to make his librettists give him real human characters to depict in music. We see here how the

122

subject of opera has shifted from mythology to history, from Greece to Rome. Nero and Poppaea are very human people, and the music has an intensity of passion that almost foreshadows *Tristan*. Monteverdi's madrigals had shown plainly that he was determined to carry voluptuous expression to its furthest limits. The later Venetian operas deal with what pretend to be historical subjects, but they really know only two emotions, ambition and desire. The French operas of Lully amounted to much the same thing, although they were better constructed and maintained a higher literary standard; both Boileau and Salvator Rosa point their satire against the operas, where everything turned on *gloire* and *amour*.

The Venetian opera, being a commercial concern, aimed at giving pleasure, and Venice was a city where morals were extremely free. It was from Venice, or more probably from Italy altogether, that the fundamental principle of all operatic morality originated – that the only motive power of drama is 'love', and that everything else has to be sacrificed to it. We have become so used to this in opera now that most people probably never worry themselves about the moral aspect of operatic love affairs; it has become a mere convention of the stage. But in Venice of the seventeenth century the opera was not so far removed from life. We may laugh at an opera about Mutius Scaevola in which he puts his hand into the fire for love, and then joins in a frivolous scene about love being a gambling game, but some of the opera plots, though they read like Shakespearean comedy gone mad, were based on things that might happen every day. The plots, it may be remarked, are incredibly complicated, and, as in *Trovatore*, a great deal of the story takes place before the curtain rises. M. Prunières, in his life of Cavalli, gives the following admirably concise summary of a typical Venetian opera, *La Constanza di Rosmonda* (1659), words by Aurelio Aureli, music by Giambattista Volpe, called Rovettino, a pupil of Cavalli.

Agamemnon loves Rosmonda, wife of Pelops, Duke of Argos, without being aware that his own son Orestes is in love with her, too. Orestes, in order to approach her, disguises himself as a statue in her garden, and is obliged to stand there motionless while he watches his

123

father attempt to seduce her. Orestes meets a young stranger and accepts him as his page; the stranger is Cyrene, a princess whom he has himself seduced, in disguise. Clytemnestra falls in love with the page. Pelops returns and suspects his wife of having affairs with three lovers, Agamemnon, Orestes and the page; in fact he actually catches the page in his wife's embraces, only to discover that the page is a woman. And Pelops is himself in disguise at this moment, for in order to trap his wife he has got himself up as a blackamoor, and Agamemnon hears to his horror that Rosmonda has been seen in the arms of a Negro. At the end Rosmonda's virtue is vindicated and Orestes marries Cyrene.

All this sounds very absurd, but take each episode singly, and it might have happened any day in Venice, except the business of the statue; Moors were not unknown there, and ladies frequently dressed in male attire for various reasons. And just as in the Shakespearean theatre women in male attire are prevalent because boys acted female parts, so in the Venetian operas the male soprano was acting male parts and often female parts as well. At Rome no women were allowed to act, and all female parts were taken by *castrati*.

The summary of *Rosmonda* given above makes no mention of the comic episodes, which were plentiful in all the Venetian operas. In the eighteenth century some sort of order was brought into librettos by Zeno and Metastasio, but some of Handel's operas have plots not unlike that of *Rosmonda*. The reform was due to the general admiration for Racine. A German producer quite recently pointed out to me the resemblance of certain Handel operas to Shakespearean comedies; English readers may think this blasphemous, but the foregoing pages will have shown that there must have been a common source.

Racine or Shakespeare? That was the fundamental problem of opera librettists for the next two centuries. Should the opera be concentrated on heroic emotions, on personal reactions, on the events of twenty-four hours, so as to crowd all these things into the closest possible space and thereby intensify them to the utmost? Or should time and place be free, the story treated more as a chronicle, with more visible action and less discussion of it, and with more liberty to introduce non-heroic characters, the picturesque and the comic?

124

Shakespeare does not make his appearance in opera until towards the end of the eighteenth century. As all opera was mainly Italian, with a certain amount of French, it was only natural that operatic poets should follow the path of Racine, though in opera there was always a third factor, that of pure spectacle. In the eighteenth century there was more restraint in the matter of spectacle, because, audiences were becoming more musical. Singers were beginning to count for more than architects. The new problem that was interesting the scene-painters was one that had little bearing on the construction of the opera as a whole; it was a question of pictorial composition. The baroque period was giving way to the rococo, and in the theatre that meant a change from an architect's vision to that of a painter. There was still plenty of imitation architecture on the stage, but it now began studiously to avoid the symmetry of the seventeenth century.

The drama of *Ambleto,* written by Apostolo Zeno in collaboration with Pietro Pariati, was set by Gasparini for Venice in 1705; it was given in London in 1712 with the famous Nicolino Grimaldi as Hamlet. It bears little resemblance to Shakespeare, of whom Zeno doubtless had never even heard the name; it is derived directly from Saxo Grammaticus, the original source of the story. Gertrude is called Gerilda, but the other characters, Hamlet excepted, have quite different names. In 1761 a comic opera called *Georget et Georgette* was produced in Paris with music by one Alexandre, based on *The Tempest*, or rather on Shadwell's adaptation of the Dryden–Davenant version; the scenes utilized do not occur in Shakespeare at all. The same year saw another comic opera adapted from *The Merry Wives of Windsor*, which had only one performance. The first play of Shakespeare ever acted in France was *Hamlet* (1769) in the version of Ducis. The next was *Romeo and Juliet* (1772), and in 1792 Monvel, who had acted in this performance, wrote the words of an opera on the same subject for Dalayrac. Needless to say, the opera had a happy end. *Romeo and Juliet* formed the basis of several operas about this time; Felice Romani's libretto was set by Vaccai in 1827 and by Bellini in 1833. Salieri wrote a *Falstaff* for Vienna in 1798 which has considerable merit. Rossini's *Otello* (Venice, 1818) was one of his most famous operas, but has not been staged for a very long time. Romani also wrote a libretto on *Hamlet* for Mercadante (Milan, 1822), with an interesting preface in which he called *Hamlet* the *Oresteia* of the North, and compares the Queen to Clytemnestra. But most of these adapters knew Shakespeare only through French versions, generally those of Ducis, who made no attempt to translate Shakespeare, but completely re-wrote some of his plays in conformity with French taste and tradition.

Romani was a man of fine literary sense, and his librettos all have considerable distinction. He realized that the problem of his time was to get rid of recitative as much as possible and to make the greatest use of ensembles. It must be remembered that he began his career at a time when the old-fashioned opera consisting almost entirely of solos with interminable *secco* recitatives was not yet dead. The trouble was that the new scheme of Italian opera derived from French models was just as conventional in its way as that of Metastasio; each principal singer had to have the right number of important songs, and each act had to end with an elaborate finale. At Paris the ballet was indispensable, and the ballet had generally to come in the third or fourth act. All these operas, whether of the French or the Italian type, become very much alike; we can see that even in the operas which have survived to our own day, and there were hundreds more that have been forgotten.

German comic opera took its librettos either from Italy or from France; many of Goldoni's librettos were translated into German. It was mainly the French librettos that served as models for the Germans in the romantic days, especially those of the 'rescue operas'. But the Germans were clumsy translators, and when they wrote original librettos they were often hampered by two habits that they never could shake off. One was their insistence on a high moral tone; this was derived from the operas of the French Revolution, and the Germans, probably from a desire to appeal to the respectable middle classes, strewed their operas with what we should call 'copybook sentiments'. It was not surprising that Wagner should inveigh against conventional librettos when those he knew best were almost all translations from Italian and French.

The other trouble of the Germans was their fondness for ballad metres. Just as the Italians wanted to get rid of *secco* recitative, so the Germans wanted to reduce the amount of spoken dialogue; but it was a grave mistake to replace it with rhymed quatrains. The Italians managed the matter more ingeniously; from Bellini to Puccini they adopted the method of letting the orchestra play a continuous piece of music, against which a rapid conversation could take place. It had the perfectly natural effect of people talking while music is going on, and the Italians wrote just the right kind of background music for it – it sometimes is actually the music being played at a party on the stage.

Wagner began with more or less conventional librettos, that is, he used conventional metres and forms. *Lohengrin* suffers from metrical monotony, and it also suffers from the fact that most of it goes at what Wagner himself called the 'German *andante*', which is the normal breathing rate of a corpulent man. It runs, or rather saunters, all through the German music of the nineteenth century. What was new in *Tannhäuser* and *Lohengrin* was the disregard of convention in the plots themselves. Tannhäuser behaves rather like Max in *Der Freischüz*, and the end, as in that opera, is neither tragic nor happy, but merely uncomfortable. The end of *Lohengrin* is more uncomfortable still, and the beginning hardly intelligible. Wagner treats some of his characters very inconsiderately from a practical point of view; in the first act of *Lohengrin* Ortrud is on the stage the whole time, and has nothing to sing except a very subordinate part in an ensemble. It has been said that a really great Ortrud can be acting all the time, but she has practically no opportunity of acting in conjunction with other characters – she can only 'register emotion'. In *Parsifal* the hero has to stand perfectly still in a corner throughout the Grail scene until he is pushed out by Gurnemanz; here, as in the second act of *The Mastersingers,* the ensemble is built up and then interrupted, but the musical construction is in *Parsifal* not so happily balanced. In the third act it is Kundry who has to remain silent; she is on the stage the whole time, and sings two words only. It is hardly surprising that the old-fashioned *prima donna* did not like Wagner; and in 1897 an old gentleman said to me that he had come out (at Covent Garden) after the second act of *Siegfried*. 'Never so bored in my life; why, there's not a female in the piece!'

127

Paris had set the example of spectacular opera under Meyer-beer, and the rolling ship in *L'Africaine* was long regarded as a marvel of stage machinery. Wagner made much greater demands on the theatre, and for a long time Bayreuth was the only place where they were fulfilled. *The Ring* began with a scene in the depths of the Rhine; this had been anticipated by a British composer, Wallace, in *Lurline* (London, 1860). The problem here was how the three Rhine-maidens were to swim. At the first performance each one was supported in the middle on an iron framework rather like a collapsible music stand; this was mounted on a small truck pushed about the stage by two men, the truck being concealed by rocks in front. The Rhine-maidens are now hung from above on a system of wires, each controlled by four men. The transformation scenes were another problem, and Wagner's demand that Alberich should become alternately invisible and visible by means of the *Tarnhelm*. For this purpose Wagner invented the steam curtain; steam was released from a row of jets along the line of the footlights, which gave it whatever colour was desired – generally pink; behind this curtain of steam a black curtain was let down until the scene had been changed. The steam was also used to hide Alberich on the stage, and to represent the flames which surrounded Brünnhilde. Its installation at Covent Garden in 1897 was a matter of some difficulty and the steam was supplied at first from a traction-engine standing in Floral Street.

Another Wagnerian innovation was the use of scenery that moved sideways. After the murder of Siegfried in *The Twilight of the Gods* clouds were to cover the scene; they came on from one side, very slowly; first just a few small thin ones, then a gradual thickening until the stage was completely hidden, the cloth being mounted on two vertical rollers, one on each side of the stage. The same device was used for the transformation in *Parsifal*, where Wagner wanted the scene of the forest to change imperceptibly into a mass of rock and then into the hall of the Grail, while Parsifal remarks,

I scarcely move, yet swiftly seem to run.

to which Gurnemanz replies,

My son, thou seest, here Space and Time are one.

128

In most theatres today the 'space–time continuum' has been dropped in favour of a plain curtain. The realistic designs which Wagner himself so much admired and which were kept up for many years at Bayreuth, besides being copied elsewhere, are now considered old-fashioned, and Wagner's problems have to be faced in a new way.

Another difficulty was the large number of animals required. Wagner's menagerie was probably suggested to him in early youth by reading the fairy plays of Carlo Gozzi (1722–1806), which are full of monsters, animals and talking birds of all kinds. The libretto of *The Magic Flute* owes a good deal to Gozzi, whose plays were translated into German during his own lifetime; Wagner's first opera, *Die Feen*, is directly based on Gozzi, and many other composers have utilized his plots. In *The Valkyrie* Fricka used to drive on in a chariot drawn by two property rams, much to the amusement of the audience. A bear comes on in *Siegfried*, and also a dragon; ravens fly up in *The Twilight of the Gods*, and a swan is shot by

Parsifal. Most important, too, was Brünnhilde's horse, which was expected to leap into the blazing funeral pyre of Siegfried with Brünnhilde on its back; many readers will remember the decrepit cab-horse at Covent Garden and how it always

129

tried to eat the scenery. The modern stage shirks as much of
the Wagnerian zoo as it can, and at Sadler's Wells poor Lohengrin has even been deprived of his swan.

New designs for *The Ring* were made about 1896 by

Adolphe Appia, a Swiss artist, but they were not officially
approved, and it is only recently that their imaginative quality
has been recognized. It would not have been possible to exe-
cute them in the old-fashioned theatre; but modern lighting
systems and the use of the cyclorama have revolutionized
stage mechanism. Another notable improvement came with
the installation of the revolving stage, originally invented by
the Japanese in the eighteenth century, but first erected in
Europe by Karl Lautenschläger at the Residenz-Theater in
Munich (1896) expressly for the purpose of producing *Don
Giovanni* without intervals between the scenes. In modern
stage mechanism Germany has always led the way, and it has
always been opera rather than drama which provided the opportunities for its display. Indeed, the German stage directors
were so proud of their machinery that they would use it even
in an opera like *La Bohème* which really needed no mechanical
effects at all.

Wagner's ideas of staging were naturally those of his own
time, and it is not surprising that they have now become old-

fashioned; none the less it is entirely to Wagner's initiative that we owe the modern developments of stage machinery, and what is of far greater consequence, the modern doctrine that every opera ought to be staged with as much care and thought as a Wagnerian music-drama.

To Wagner also we owe the general improvement in the standard of operatic acting, although the habitual play-goer is inclined to consider all operatic acting ridiculous. An opera singer's only idea of acting he would say, is to stand at the footlights in the middle of the stage and wave his arms alternately. The late Mr J. A. Fuller Maitland, a former musical critic of *The Times*, told me that he had seen a very amusing case of this in Germany at a performance of an opera in which the hero has to come on with one of his arms in a sling – *Das Goldene Kreuz*, by Ignaz Brüll; the singer, accustomed to wave his arms alternately, was dreadfully embarrassed by the sling, as he could only wave one. After some awkward movements he finally solved the problem by taking the 'wounded' arm out of the sling when its turn came, waving it, and then putting it back in the sling while he waved the other.

This arm-waving is a gesture which probably goes back to the days of Cicero or earlier, and, to judge from old pictures, it was the standard gesture of actors in what we now call the 'barnstorming' days. On the operatic stage it was natural enough, for singers find that it helps the emission of the voice, and, according to Wagner, this movement was conventionalized and made seemly by the ballet dancers. It is highly probable that the style of acting practised by the best operatic actors in the early nineteenth century was derived from the ballet rather than from the playhouse; for one thing, it was the period of the great dramatic ballets initiated by Noverre, and secondly, operatic acting must of necessity differ from ordinary acting because it has to be synchronized with music.

It is evident that it must have taken some time for any systematic principles of operatic acting to emerge. The stage directions from the earliest operas which I have quoted in this chapter show the close connexion with the ballet, and also suggest that early opera singers were hardly expected to act at all. For over two hundred years the criticism of opera concerns itself almost exclusively with the singing. There

131

certainly were dramatic singers in those days, but what critics – Dr Burney, for example – looked for was dramatic expression in the singing voice. Madame Mara, one of the greatest singers of the eighteenth century (1749–1833), was much admired by Goethe's friend Zelter when she sang a certain air of Graun 'with a voice of tremendous power, and with a maternal pathos that forced bitter tears from my eyes every time I heard her; it was as if a thousand nightingales were straining their throats to warble for revenge'. Mara was censured by some of the critics for her want of action in passionate parts. 'What!' she used to exclaim, 'am I to sing with my hands and legs? I am a singer, and what I cannot do with my voice I will not do at all.'

On the other hand, Nicolini, 'the first truly great singer who had ever sung in our theatre', according to Dr Burney, won high praise from Steele in *The Tatler* for his acting in Scarlatti's *Pyrrhus and Demetrius* (1708).

Every limb and every finger contributes to the part he acts, in so much that a deaf man may go along with him in the sense of it. There is scarce a beautiful posture in an old statue which he does not plant himself in, as the different circumstances of the story give occasion for it.

But eighteenth-century opera, with its alternation of recitative and air, inevitably imposed a certain conventionality on acting. The formal shape of the airs precluded any sort of realistic acting during their performance, though occasionally, as in Scarlatti's *Griselda* (1722), there might be a special 'dramatic' air consisting mainly of short exclamations addressed to two other characters alternately, here the heroine's little son and the tyrant who is on the point of slaying him. Acting, in the ordinary sense, would be confined to her recitatives.

During the next hundred years or so we find records of various individual singers, generally female, who were admired for their dramatic interpretations, but in almost all cases it was the dramatic singing rather than the acting which impressed the critics. Mme Milder, for whom Beethoven wrote the part of Leonora in *Fidelio*, was admired for her attitudes and the arrangement of her draperies. Mme Schröder-Devrient, the Leonora of the following generation, threw herself into all her parts with an appalling sincerity, but was not really a good singer. Mme Malibran (d. 1836) was a great singer with immense vitality rather than technical skill in acting. The comic operas of that period, and especially the French romantic operas, must have called for plenty of normal acting; but that took place only during the spoken dialogue. Anything like team-work in operatic acting must have been excessively rare, though possibly the famous quartet of Grisi, Mario, Tamburini and Lablache achieved it at Paris in the 1840s.

When we consider the wide range of period and style covered by the standard repertory, it is astonishing how successful modern singers are in adapting themselves to such various requirements. An opera of Gluck demands statuesque poses and conventionalized movements; *Louise* calls for everyday realism. It is hardly possible to arrive at any system of basic principles. There is at any rate one generally accepted standard rule : to remain still while actually singing, and to make one's movements between the vocal phrases. The part of Susanna in *The Marriage of Figaro* illustrates this very well. More movement may be allowed in recitative, and it may be even indispensable at certain isolated moments. Producers, especially in Germany, where much trouble is taken about production and theories always precede practice, have sometimes gone to extremes in laying down the law. The old-fashioned Italian singer always came down to the footlights and took advantage of the broad apron; German producers rigidly forbade their singers to cross the line of the tableau curtains, and under the influence of the Meiningen Shakespeare productions they made every chorus singer act an individual part, which was sometimes very distracting. A reaction against this set in with the Handel revival; one producer of Handel's operas made his singers bow or curtsey to the audience before and after every single song.

In spoken drama, one of the most difficult things to achieve is skilful timing of words and actions, and the general pace at which a scene has to move. In opera all this is automatically regulated by the music, whether a character is singing or not; the difficulty which most often arises is that of slowing down action to the pace of the orchestra. This is very noticeable in Wagner's later operas. Wagner himself knew exactly what he wanted in the way of movement and gesture; and every action had to be synchronized exactly with the music. In a Wagner opera, and in many others, such as Saint Saëns' *Samson and Delilah*, the singer ought to time every gesture so as to make the audience think that it is his inward emotion which causes the orchestra to play the appropriate musical phrase. What generally happens is that when the orchestra plays the phrase the singer is caught napping and suddenly remembers that he has some gesture to make at this point – half a bar too late.

One reason why operatic acting has often been so distressing is that many singers belong to a social class very different from that of the average modern actor. A hundred years ago or more both actors and singers were more or less 'rogues and vagabonds'. Today the drama is plentifully supplied with young people of good education and quick intelligence. Singers are not so easy to pick up; fine voices often come from Yorkshire mills and Welsh mines. Even in Handel's day it is remarkable how many famous singers were notorious for their ugliness, and all through the nineteenth century opera singers were a by-word for ungainly figures. Schnorr von Carolsfeld and his wife, the first Tristan and Isolde, were both monstrously fat.

The singing voice often takes some years to develop, and it is extremely rare for either men or women of about nineteen to be able to undertake big operatic parts, whereas they might easily make a success as Romeo or Juliet. Moreover, the public demands singers of established reputation in the famous operas, and indeed hardly realizes the moral repulsiveness of a Don Giovanni who looks well over fifty. Fortunately, the tendency of the present day, at any rate in England, is for the more intelligent audiences to prefer team-work and sensitive understanding to mere enormity of voice, so that a more generous appreciation is forthcoming for singers who, if not up to the standards, vocal and physical, of the grand Wagnerian manner, are at any rate reasonably able to look the parts they represent. And it is also the tendency at the present day to produce opera more and more in the spirit of ballet. Opera, by virtue of its music, stands nearer to ballet than to drama, even to poetic drama. Wagner, when he wrote that operatic gesture was derived from ballet, was expressing his contempt for both,

134

but although Wagner had a natural distaste for admitting his indebtedness to earlier musicians, it is obvious that the Wagnerian system of acting could never have come into existence but for the dramatic ballets of Noverre. And the modern ballet, as exemplified by Kurt Jooss's *Chronica*, has become so serious and tragic that modern Wagnerian production may well seek to learn something from it.

CHAPTER NINE

MODERN OPERA – RICHARD STRAUSS – DEBUSSY –
BUSONI – HINDEMITH – KURT WEILL – PIZZETTI

It was only natural that after the deaths of Wagner and Verdi
many critics should have proclaimed that opera was played
out. A few attempts were made in Germany to carry on the
grand Wagnerian manner, but none of these imitations have
kept the stage. As a curiosity we may mention August Bungert,
who round about 1900 composed a cycle of six operas dealing
with stories from Homer, and even proposed that a special
theatre on the lines of Bayreuth should be erected for him on
the banks of the Rhine. The most conspicuous figure in Germany since Wagner has been Richard Strauss (b. 1864), who
has evolved his own way of dealing with 'music-drama'. Strauss
began his career with chamber music of a very classical turn;
the first of his symphonic poems, *Don Juan*, appeared in 1888,
and *Ein Heldenleben*, the last of the series, ten years later. A
very Wagnerian opera, *Guntram*, came out in 1894, but his
first real success in the theatre was the comic opera *Feuersnot*
(Dresden, 1901); it is amusing, but rather coarse, and suffers
to some extent from a tendency to preach at the audience
about Wagner and Strauss himself – this was perhaps more
the fault of the librettist. In 1905 Strauss created a far greater
scandal by his setting of Oscar Wilde's play, *Salome* (Dresden,
1905); some people considered the play itself revolting, but far
more were repelled by the music, which seemed then uncompromisingly modern. Nowadays its dissonances are not particu-

136

larly frightening, but *Salome* is of historic importance as the foundation of the 'modern' style in Germany. The orchestra is treated with astonishing virtuosity; the voice parts are angular and unmelodious, based on a violent and exaggerated declamation. In addition, the characters of the play are almost all perversely unpleasant, and this is very skilfully reflected in their music; it is said that Strauss originally conceived of John the Baptist as a grotesque figure, too, but saw that he must be made sympathetic in order to contrast with the others. Unfortunately, the composer's only idea of 'sympathetic' music was the kind usually associated with German beer-gardens; and the whole of Strauss's musical output has been disfigured by fatal lapses into this German *bourgeois* style. *Salome* was followed by *Elektra* (Dresden, 1909), which was considered in every way more repulsive than its predecessor; at the present day it is recognized that much of it is genuinely beautiful, and many people regard it as the composer's best work.

Strauss continued to make more and more extravagant demands on the orchestra, and displayed an incredible virtuosity in writing descriptive music for the orchestra. These two operas show also his technique of 'music-drama'; he did not write his own librettos, but took over practically without alteration plays which had already been acted without music, plays, too, which were outstanding works of literature. *Elektra* was by Hofmannsthal, who continued to collaborate with Strauss up to his death. They were not really a very well assorted pair, for Strauss's chief quality has always been a robust energy and sensual exuberance; his later career shows that the 'perversities' of *Salome* and *Elektra* were artificial studies in technique. Hofmannsthal, on the other hand, was a Viennese aristocrat with a Jewish strain, the product of an over-refined and delicate culture derived largely from French and Italian sources. In *Der Rosenkavalier* (Dresden, 1911) he wrote his play as a libretto for Strauss, but it still remains too much of a play and too much overladen with minute details to make a really good opera. The detail at any rate offered Strauss opportunities for ingenuity, though these things all delayed the progress of the drama; still more to Strauss's taste was the unabashed eroticism of the story, and the rather revolting, though

extremely comic, figure of the gross and elderly *roué*, Baron
Ochs. When the work was first performed in Vienna the
subscribers of the opera were horrified by the fact that most
of the libretto was in broad Viennese dialect; it was more or
less exactly the language that the imperial court of Vienna
habitually spoke, but to hear actors speak it on the stage of the
imperial court opera gave them a shock.

A new Strauss opera invariably meant something startling,
and the next experiment was indeed curious; Hofmannsthal
translated Molière's *Le Bourgeois Gentilhomme*, which was
acted as a play, but as a play with ballets, exactly as was intended by Molière. For this Strauss wrote ballet music based
on Lully's original music, and as an epilogue the opera *Ariadne
on Naxos*, the idea of Hofmannsthal being that Monsieur
Jourdain, having ordered both an opera and a comedy of
masks for the entertainment of his guests, suddenly decides
to have them both performed simultaneously. The first performance of this work was given at Stuttgart (1912) in the
small house of the newly erected court theatre, which included
two theatres of different sizes. The orchestra was proportion-
ately small, but Strauss managed to make it sound marvellously
noisy. The opera was bewildering to anyone not prepared for
it beforehand. *Arianna* by itself was intended to suggest something like Monteverdi's *Ariadne* of 1608, with long mono-
logues for Ariadne, assisted by attendant nymphs, until the
arrival of Bacchus; this, however, has to be interrupted by the
entrances of the Italian mask figures, Zerbinetta and four
buffoons. Strauss was quite content to let them sing male-
voice part-songs in the old German style; the chief novelty
was a *coloratura* part for Zerbinetta that was more difficult
than anything ever written before. Eventually the whole piece
was remodelled; Molière's play was dropped, and the sub-
stance of it, in so far as it introduced *Ariadne*, turned into a
first act of the opera. The work as now performed is completely inconsequent, but has a good deal of musical charm
and offers great opportunities to the stage decorator.

The *Legend of Joseph* (Paris, 1914) was a ballet, produced
by Diaghilev, in which Massine made his first appearance. Another opera, *The Woman Without a Shadow* (Vienna, 1919),
was Hofmannsthal's ideal of a new *Magic Flute*, as *Rosen-*

kavalier had been a sort of new *Marriage of Figaro*. Strauss had made a name for himself in the 1890s as a conductor of Mozart at Munich; but his most ardent admirers could hardly find much that was Mozartian in his own works. This new opera, which required immense stage resources, was a very complicated fairy-tale, in which the 'shadow' symbolized motherhood; like the episode of Papageno and Papagena in *The Magic Flute*, it proclaims the duty of fecundity. A special performance of it was given by the Vienna Opera at Venice in 1934 shortly after the official publication of a stirring article attributed to Mussolini himself, on the encouragement of the Italian birthrate.

Another ballet, *Schlagobers (Whipped Cream,* Vienna, 1924), caused some scandal, as the Viennese journalists took offence at an episode which was interpreted as being anti-semitic. More amusing was the comic opera *Intermezzo* (Vienna, 1925), for which Strauss wrote the words himself; it deals with a domestic episode alleged to be founded on facts of the composer's own private life. It was really something new in opera – a series of little scenes, all in modern dress, including tobogganing in Switzerland and a careful representation of Strauss's own favourite card game, Skat. The score is full of musical jokes of all kinds, but few listeners would recognize them in performance. *The Egyptian Helen* (Dresden, 1928), a serious opera to a libretto by Hofmannsthal, did not seem to contain much that was new. The last opera written for Strauss by Hofmannsthal before his death was *Arabella* (Dresden, 1933), a comedy about social life in Vienna in 1860. The libretto would make a charming play by itself, and is written with great delicacy; Strauss, always with grand opera in his mind, never quite catches the natural conversational tone of the words. After Wagner, composers began to feel that librettos ought to stand at least on the same literary level as plays; but frightened, perhaps, by the accusation brought against Wagner that he showed no consideration for voices, they treated these literary librettos with little more respect than their predecessors of the century before. Strauss evidently took pleasure in the sound of singing, and that led him to prolong single syllables to an exaggerated extent; the device appears to show off the voices, but it makes the words unintelligible. When *Der Rosenkavalier* was recently produced at Sadler's Wells, a critic amusingly called it an 'opera without words'; the fault lay neither with the singers nor with the translator (the late Mr Alfred Kalisch), but with Strauss himself, for the way in which he had set them.

Another post-Wagnerian of modern Germany must be mentioned, although his music is very little known in this country – Hans Pfitzner (b. 1869), whose music descends partly from Schumann and partly from *Parsifal*. Pfitzner first made his name with *Der arme Heinrich* (Mainz, 1895), a morbidly painful treatment of the story familiar to English readers as *The Golden Legend* (Longfellow); his most interesting work is *Palestrina* (Munich, 1917), an opera on a huge scale dealing with the famous Italian composer, who in the first act composes a mass to the dictation of a choir of angels. The second act is a masterly representation of the Council of Trent, such as Meyerbeer himself might have planned. *Palestrina*, like *Parsifal*, is what is called a 'festival opera', which means that it is intended to begin about five o'clock in the afternoon and go on till eleven, with intervals for meals. It is dreadfully tedious, but it has much that is wonderfully beautiful, and its lofty idealism compels sincere respect. The libretto is by Pfitzner himself, and is rather clumsily written.

Strauss and Puccini are the only composers of recent times whose operas have taken undisputed possession of the stage and won international acceptance. Apart from them, the modern history of opera shows complete confusion. Some writers have said that the day of opera is at an end, and that modern political conditions have made it an impossible form of art. That is not borne out by the facts. But political events have changed the quality of audiences, for economic reasons; and while composers are anxious to break with traditional routine, managers are shy of trying experiments and prefer to stick to a safe orthodox repertory, not perhaps realizing that the public is rapidly tiring of some of the 'old favourites'. We need not waste time here on the purely commercial composers; but there are a few works which, although not permanent popular successes, have left their mark on the development of modern opera.

The first of these in time was Debussy's (1862–1918) *Pel-*

léas et Mélisande (Paris, 1902), a setting of the play by Maeterlinck. Maeterlinck himself disapproved violently of the opera, but the evident reason was that Debussy had given the heroine's part to Mary Garden instead of to Maeterlinck's wife. In those days Maeterlinck himself was considered unintelligible by the ordinary Philistine; Debussy's music seemed merely to aggravate that character of elusiveness, and the opera was received by most critics with bitter hostility. It was conceived as a deliberate refutation of Wagnerian principles, and it could never have been written but for Wagner. The words all through are more spoken than sung, and this recitative, instead of following the grand manner of Lully and Rameau, is made to sound as much as possible like modern spoken French, the French of conversation, and very restrained conversation, rather than that of the stage. Much of it is almost monotone. It is accompanied by vague sounds that seem to have no musical connexion, sounds overheard rather than heard, dim backgrounds of half-suggested feelings. The strain of listening to this rather long opera, almost all in subdued tones, never knowing what the harmonies of the music are, never knowing what the characters are really supposed to be thinking and doing, until at the end Mélisande dies, and the watchers round the bed suddenly fall on their knees, is to some people unbearable. After a short period of notoriety, when the opera was performed in all the principal opera houses, even in Germany and Italy, *Pelléas et Mélisande* was for a time almost completely forgotten, but it has been revived recently in Paris and elsewhere, and seems now to be firmly established as a standard classic of the French repertory. Connoisseurs maintain that it can be acted in no language except French; but if there is one other language in which it is possible, it is English. Outside France, and even there, it may not be a work for the multitude; but it is certainly one of those masterpieces which have a profound reward for those who are willing to surrender themselves to the contemplation of it.

Pelléas et Mélisande was an experiment that could never be repeated, and it could hardly be said to have formed a school. But its influence can be traced on later composers; it helped to set them free from Wagnerism on the one hand and Puccinism on the other, and for those who had ears to hear

141

it, it carried a message of pure idealism. Such operas as Willem Pijper's *Sieur Halewyn* (Amsterdam, 1933), Manuel de Falla's *El Amor Brujo* (Madrid, 1915), and Béla Bartók's *Duke Bluebeard's Castle* (Frankfurt, 1922) all show the new outlook. Bartók's opera especially reminds us of Debussy's in its sense of remoteness from life; it is not in the least French, as the libretto is written in a Hungarian ballad metre which gives it a very definite rhythmical character of its own.

Among the French composers of opera the most notable is Darius Milhaud (b. 1892), whose *Christophe Colomb* (Berlin, 1930), to a libretto by Paul Claudel, employed a vast apparatus, with a lecturer and responsive chorus in front of the stage, and cinema effects alternating with acted scenes. It is a very impressive work, but very difficult to put on the stage, and belongs to the class of operas which one does not expect to see more than once or twice in a lifetime.

Ferruccio Busoni (1866-1924), remembered chiefly as a marvellous pianist, composed four operas; although they were all written to German words by Busoni himself, they show descent from Verdi's *Falstaff* rather than from Wagner, to whose methods Busoni in later life was vehemently opposed. *Die Brautwahl* (Hamburg, 1912) bewildered its audiences by its distracting wealth of ideas, and the composer forgot, as others had done before him, that an audience cannot be expected to know the whole story beforehand. Much more successful were two short comic operas, *Turandot* and *Arlecchino* (Zürich, 1917), both of which are extremely witty and amusing. His last opera, *Doctor Faust* (Dresden, 1925), was left unfinished at his death and was completed by his Spanish pupil, Philipp Jarnach. It is based not on Goethe, but on the old puppet play of *Faust*; the libretto, written by Busoni himself, is full of mysterious meanings. Before 1933 it had come to be performed on most of the bigger stages of Germany, and was on the way to be regarded as the sort of opera to be kept for days of special solemnity. A concert performance was given in London by the B.B.C. in 1937, but it has not yet been put on the stage in this country.

The years between 1919 and 1933 were amazingly productive in Germany. The censorship was abolished, and artists rejoiced in their freedom. It soon became almost a point of honour with conductors never to give a concert without the first performance of a new work. Never had young composers such chances, and their chances were by no means limited to the concert-room. In spite of the desperate financial stringency, the opera houses were kept going, and after the inflation of the currency had once been mastered there seemed to be always plenty of money to spend on new productions. It was Berlin, not Paris, that was ready to face both the labour and the expense of Milhaud's *Christophe Colomb*. Experiments were always being tried; a good many deserved nothing more than ridicule, and a good many of the new operas produced were ephemeral in character. None the less, even the ephemeral operas were often interesting, and paved the way for further and more serious developments. Topical satire was provided by the early operas of Ernst Křenek, and more successfully in Hindemith's (b. 1895) very entertaining *Neues vom Tage (News of the Day,* Berlin, 1929). The libretto was amusingly modern, and the sensation of the opera was a scene in which the heroine, lying in a bath at a hotel, sang the praises of electric heating – 'constant hot water, no horrid smell, no danger of explosion', etc. When the work was announced for performance at Breslau the local gas company applied for, and obtained, an injunction, as this song was considered damaging to their trade. Opera is taken seriously in Germany.

Satire of a more savage type was seen in *Die Bürgschaft* (*The Surety,* Berlin, 1931), by Kurt Weill (b. 1900), pupil of Busoni; this was an elaborate opera depicting the gradual growth and consequent demoralization of an industrial town. The most sordid and at the same time the most terribly moving of all these modern German operas was Alban Berg's (1885–1935) *Wozzeck* (Berlin, 1925), based on a play by Georg Büchner, a dramatist who lived in the early part of the nineteenth century. The poignant force of this opera was incontestable, despite the utter incomprehensibility of its musical idiom to all except the initiated of the Schönberg group, and it soon found its way all over Germany, though performances were stopped in 1933.

Hungarian opera in this period was well represented by Zoltán Kodály's (b. 1882) *Háry János* (Budapest, 1926), which is almost more of a play with music than an opera. The play treats of the alleged adventures of Háry János (John Háry), an old peasant who pretends to have fought in the wars and captured Napoleon single-handed. The scenes are all presented quite fantastically, as a Hungarian peasant would imagine them, and the music consists mostly of traditional Hungarian songs and dances, with other pieces of incidental music. The whole entertainment is intensely Hungarian and full of absurd humour.

In Italy there was a small party of modernists, but they were more appreciated in other countries than in their own. Opera is a national industry in Italy and experiments are not much encouraged. Even the orthodox Ottorino Respighi (1879–1936) was mainly dependent on German theatres for the first production of his operas. He was a most accomplished eclectic, and at one time called by his countrymen 'the Strauss of Italy'; his most successful opera was *La Fiamma* (*The Flame*), founded on a Norwegian play known in England as *The Witch*, but transferred very effectively to Ravenna in the early middle ages. Respighi's knowledge of medieval church music stood him in good stead as a composer, and his opera is full of picturesque ceremonial as well as exhibiting dramatic scenes of passion.

Much more original are the operas of Ildebrando Pizzetti (b. 1880). Pizzetti in his younger days was closely associated with Gabriele d'Annunzio, who allowed him to adapt his drama, *Fedra,* as an opera (Milan, 1915); he stated publicly that Pizzetti's setting of words was always exactly in accordance with the right declamation. We see here how Boito's Shakespearean librettos had influenced the younger generation; Pizzetti was a man of literary culture and in his boyhood had been more inclined to write plays than to compose music. After this opera he turned away from d'Annunzio and found himself driven to write his own librettos. The next was taken from the Bible – *Débora e Jaèle* (Milan, 1922), and having written his own words Pizzetti felt himself more free to give rein to his lyric impulses. More successful was *Fra Gherardo* (Milan, 1928), the story of a medieval friar who yields to the temptation of a woman, repents and joins the flagellants, but meets the woman again and finds her changed like the Thaïs of Anatole France and Massenet. In *Orsèolo* (Florence, 1935) the declamatory element is preponderant, but Pizzetti has always been very successful in combining natural declamation with a melodious outline.

Francesco Malipiero (b. 1882), a descendant of an ancient and illustrious Venetian family, has been influenced in operatic composition both by his local traditions and by his research studies on Monteverdi. He has tried many original experiments in opera, but few of them have had permanent success. His trilogy *Il Mistero di Venezia*, refused by the large theatres of Italy on the ground that its scenic effects were beyond their resources, was first produced at the modest theatre of Coburg in 1933. *La Favola del Figlio Cambiato (The Changeling)*, to a brilliantly politico-satirical libretto by Pirandello, was produced at Rome in 1934, but withdrawn immediately by order of Mussolini, as it was supposed to cast ridicule on cabinet ministers, and in modern dress, too. Malipiero had more lasting success with his Shakespearean operas *Julius Caesar* (Genoa, 1936) and *Antony and Cleopatra*.

All these experimental operas have confirmed the truth that can be learned from the operas of the past – that no opera can hold the interest of an audience unless the composer gives the innermost expression of his thought to the voices on the stage. The reactions of modern German audiences might seem to contradict this, and it is undoubtedly true that many German opera-goers became so obsessed by the personality of certain conductors – thanks to the adoration lavished on them by their attendant journalists – that they paid little attention to the singers and confined all their interest to the orchestra. There were plenty, too, who cared for nothing except 'perversity' and stage machinery. In the long run those perverse-minded people do not count; the popular repertory shows that lasting success is accorded only to those operas where the voices take the lead.

The following statistics (taken from the *Allgemeine Musikzeitung*) for the German opera houses during the season 1937-8 are illuminating. The figures after each opera indicate the number of performances.

Pagliacci 354, *Cavalleria Rusticana* 352, *Madame Butterfly* 317, *Der Schwarze Peter* 298, *Czar and Zimmermann* 288, *The Bartered Bride* 286, *Il Trovatore* 267, *Carmen,* 266, *Der Freischütz* 249, *La Bohème* 238,

Lohengrin 236, *La Traviata* 236, *The Barber of Seville* 232, *Der Rosen-kavalier* 230, *Rigoletto* 226, *Aïda* 226, *Martha* 220, *Fidelio* 205, *The Mastersingers* 203, *Tosca* 201.

Schwarzer Peter, by Norbert Schulze, was a new opera at that time, intended for children; it began with the birth of a baby, and more were born of successive generations at the ends of the second and third acts. It will be noticed that Mozart does not achieve two hundred performances in Germany with any opera. Out of twenty operas listed, ten are Italian, eight are German, one Czech and one French. Only three of the twenty were written since 1900. Practically all of them belong to the popular melodious categary, though it is true that some of them were considered anti-musical when they first came out.

The eternal problem of opera is that of recitative and air. Audiences discovered soon after 1600 that they did not want to listen to operas that were all recitative; and it is equally impossible to shirk the problem of recitative and try to con-struct an opera that shall be all melodious song. If a subject is sufficiently poetical and unreal, it may be possible to evade altogether those awkward bits of informative conversation which sound so ridiculous when set to music; but the nearer an opera comes to common life, the more traps of this kind there will be for unwary composers or those without a sense of humour.

The revival of comic opera is a welcome sign. It may well seem very strange that after a period of some fifty years dur-ing which comic opera gradually ousted *opera seria* the comic opera should entirely disappear from the Italian stage. Be-tween about 1843 and 1893 there is nothing that has sur-vived, although it must be remembered that the older comic operas such as *The Barber of Seville* and *The Daughter of the Regiment* were constantly being performed. But the great majority of operas were tragic, and in almost every one the heroine, be she virtuous or a sinner, sacrifices herself for love. Wagner claimed 'redemption through love' as a monopoly of his own, but it was really the common routine of all nineteenth-century operas from Spontini's *La Vestale* onwards. Perhaps it corresponded to the universal desire of mankind; but still that does not account for the disappearance of comic opera.

As the older librettists had looked to Racine, so the more modern poetasters followed the lead of Victor Hugo. And in this connexion it is interesting to note that Alfieri (1749–1803), the chief representative of the romantic movement in Italian poetry and drama, expressed great indignation at the Italians' preference for opera rather than for tragedy, that is, for spoken tragedy. Being a writer of tragedies himself, he naturally took the view that tragedy was morally elevating, whereas he considered opera to be decadent and effeminate. No doubt this charge of effeminacy was suggested by the general admiration for the *castrati* and their *roulades*; being a man of letters and not a musician, he hardly realized that the things he was girding against were already going out of fashion without any impulse from him. Alfieri, seeing that mere indignation was not much use, proposed to bring about a compromise; he planned the construction of what he called a *tramelogedy,* in other words a tragic drama in which music should take a considerable part and be justified by its association with supernatural characters. The first act was to be opera, the second tragedy; the third and fourth were to be mixed, but the last act was to be pure tragedy. Apparently the idea was not very successful, as Alfieri did not write more than one of the six tramelogedies that he had contemplated – it was on the subject of Cain and Abel. Is it possible that the events of the early nineteenth century restored to Italy that virility which their great poet missed, and that instead of taking to spoken drama they stuck to their operas, but demanded in them a new sense of tragic intensity and strength? Might not Alfieri have changed his mind if he had been acquainted with Verdi?

One reason for the neglect of comic opera during the second half of the nineteenth century might well be that Italy at that time was too busy establishing her political position in Europe to aquire the mental equilibrium and the general social security that comedy presupposes. In our own day the fate of Malipiero's comic fairy-tale is significant.

CHAPTER TEN

OPERA IN ENGLAND – THE BEGINNINGS – LOCKE – PURCELL

THE foregoing pages have made no mention of opera in England; the reason is that English opera from the very beginning was a thing apart. In the Middle Ages the music and drama of England had not been so very different from those arts as practised on the Continent; but in the sixteenth century the English theatre began to go its own way. It was closely associated with music; dumb shows accompanied by music were a striking feature of the pre-Shakespearean drama. We might very naturally wonder why it was that Elizabethan dramatists did not combine with the Elizabethan musicians to produce operas which no other country could have equalled, all the more so as the choristers' plays of the sixteenth century do indeed show the first beginnings of the operatic idea – the use of inter-polated songs to express heightened emotions. But it is fairly clear that in Elizabethan England, as in Renaissance Italy, music was always regarded as a subservient art, however enthusiastically it might be cultivated. The history of music shows us that up to the end of the sixteenth century the church was the only place in which music could be performed on an extended scale. The longest compositions of those days are always Masses. In church people seem to have been ready to listen to an hour of music just as they were accustomed to listen to or sleep through sermons of the same length; in secular life music existed almost exclusively for entertainment, and as what is now called 'utility music'.

It was in England, towards the end of the sixteenth century, that instrumental chamber music was first cultivated – that is, music for music's sake, 'abstract music', as it was called in the days of Beethoven's string quartets. But this, like the Eng-lish madrigals, was music for private houses, although instru-mental music was certainly played in the theatres, and a great deal of it. Yet even there it had a purpose; it was played first just to pass the time while the audience was assembling, and, secondly, as an adjunct to the play. There is a fundamental difference between a collection of separate pieces by differ-ent composers brought together to serve the purpose of a play or masque, and a series composed by one man as an organic unity, designed for that particular play and for no other.

The declamatory style of singing as practised in Italy about 1600 soon became known in England; indeed, it took firmer root here than in any other country, for English people were still enjoying 'recitative musick' in the days of the Restoration, when Italy had moved on to very different things. The chief composers of recitative music – we must keep these two words together, as the technical English name for the style in those days – were the brothers Henry and William Lawes, closely connected with the court of Charles I. The obvious place for it in English life was the court masque, a species of entertainment that is neither play nor opera; it was always an imitation of the Italian entertainments, especially in its scenery and dances. One at least of the Jacobean masques was set to music all the way in this style, but unfortunately the music has not survived.

149

English travellers, like Milton and Evelyn, went to Italy and saw the new entertainments that were called operas, but it was a long time before anything like a real opera could be put on the English stage. Probably the masque was so well established by the time of James I and Charles I that there was no desire to attempt anything else; moreover, France was nearer to England than Italy, and the later masque took many of its ideas from the French *ballet de cour*. Nevertheless, D'Avenant, the author and organizer of several masques, obtained from Charles I a patent for the establishment of a theatre, and the document shows clearly that he contemplated giving not only plays, but concerts and operas in it as well. The Civil War put an end to the scheme for the moment, but D'Avenant was watching his opportunity, and in 1656 he thought it safe to make a preliminary trial with a curious entertainment, half concert, half lecture, at Rutland House (Aldersgate Street) in the City of London, to see whether there was any chance of getting the theatre reopened and plays put on the public stage again.

Cromwell and the leading Puritans had no objection at all to acting, dancing or music in themselves. They were all cultivated in the schools for boys and girls of the upper classes, and it was accepted without question that such arts were of high educational value. The cause of scandal was the public theatre and the way in which people behaved there, and it cannot be denied that the theatre, as a place of resort, has had a reputation for immorality in most countries, a reputation which has even now been not quite completely lived down. Some of the school masques have come down to us; the most interesting is *Cupid and Death,* by James Shirley, first performed in 1653. It was revived in 1659, with music by Matthew Locke 1630–77) and Christopher Gibbons (1615–75); in all probability Gibbons wrote his contributions for the earlier performance, but how much else belonged to it can only be conjectured. It is a play in a series of scenes, with musical interludes sung by two soloists and a chorus; probably that was its earliest form. In 1656 D'Avenant brought out his first English opera, *The Siege of Rhodes,* followed in 1658 and 1659 by two more experiments in that field. Locke was closely associated with these, so in all probability what he did with *Cupid and*

Death in 1659 was to add a good deal more music, setting as recitative some scenes which had previously been spoken, so as to make it more like a real opera.

D'Avenant's chief motive was to get the theatres reopened, and his own plays performed. *The Siege of Rhodes* must have been planned originally as an ordinary play; it is not in the least like any Italian opera, either in subject or construction, nor has it any ascertainable French model. It was performed in 1656 at Rutland House; the hall was said to be large enough for 400 people, but the stage was absurdly small, being 18 feet wide (proscenium opening), 9 feet high (with a frieze of 2 feet above) and about 15 feet deep. The designs for the scenery have been preserved; they were made by John Webb, a pupil of Inigo Jones.

The subject of the opera is the siege of Rhodes, then held by the Knights of St John, and its capture by Solyman the Magnificent in 1522, but the siege itself is merely the background for imaginary episodes which the author hoped would 'advance the characters of virtue in the shapes of valour and conjugal love'. It is in five acts, called 'entries', no doubt in order to suggest that it was a masque and not a play; each ends with a chorus of some sort. There is only one actual song in the whole opera; the rest is all in dialogue, set to music as recitative. The music, which was by Locke and others, has been lost, and so has that of the two operas which followed. The performance must have been very much of a makeshift, and it is evident that the original play had to be much cut down.

The scenery consisted of three pairs of wings representing rocks; these remained unchanged throughout the opera. At the back there were changeable scenes painted on two flats; there were four pairs of these, each 9 feet wide. On these were painted various views; the audience does not seem to have worried about the vertical line of junction, and the system was carried on in England even in the nineteenth century, at any rate in the humbler theatres. One scene represented Mount Philermus, with a castle, and the Turkish army in the plain below; the painter had no scruple about showing painted groups of human beings engaged in violent action.

The next opera, *The Cruelty of the Spaniards in Peru,* was

151

altogether more like a lecture. There were six scenes, each introduced by appropriate instrumental music; each scene was explained by the High Priest of Peru, after which there followed a song and a dumb show with dancing, of course to appropriate music. This is more like pantomime ballet than like opera. The entertainment in this way presented the whole history of Peru, beginning with the age of primitive happiness and ending with a prophetic vision of the Spaniards being expelled by Peruvians with the help of the English. *The History of Sir Francis Drake* is more like *The Siege of Rhodes,* and is definitely a drama, though with curious limitations. The scene is laid in Peru and Panama. In one act Drake is shown a beautiful lady who has been captured by savages and tied to a tree; but as there was some fear of trouble with the authorities, the bride was represented only by a painted canvas. No woman took part in this opera, although *The Siege of Rhodes* had seen the first appearance of any woman (Mrs Coleman) on the public stage in England.

After the Restoration there was no more need for pretence, and D'Avenant was able to produce *The Siege of Rhodes,* and a sequel to it as well, as plays with women in the female parts. How much of the music was kept is not known. For the moment all idea of opera was abandoned, but it was soon seen that some of Shakespeare's plays required a good deal of music and might well be given more. England was gradually adopting the new Italian type of picture-frame stage, and scenery now began to be an important item in the production of Shakespeare. The plays that best suited the new taste were *The Tempest* and *Macbeth,* the latter not so much on account of the heroic title part as for the opportunities given by the witches for singing and especially for flying. Flying was the latest novelty in stage effect, and audiences seem to have found it a great attraction.

The year 1674 saw several operatic adventures in London. To begin with (I make no attempt at chronological order, as the exact dates of these performances are uncertain), there was *Ariane,* a French opera by Cambert and Grabu, performed in honour of the marriage of the Duke of York with Mary of Modena. The preface to the libretto apologizes for its feebleness, and for that of the translation, too, 'the *Original* itself being ... only a bare *Collection of Phrases*, and *Expressions* made fit for *Sound* and *Harmony*; ... and, were both much worse than they are, the Pomp and Magnificence of its *Representation* will alone prove sufficient to plead their excuse'. This seems to have been our first taste of imported opera.

Native opera was represented by *Psyche*, words by Thomas Shadwell, music by Locke. The libretto is an adaptation of Molière's *Psyché*, for which Lully had written music; but Shadwell had his own ideas of what an English opera ought to be. He has such a bad reputation among men of letters that it is only just to his memory to say that he was a keen amateur musician – something of a composer, in fact – and had the makings of an admirable librettist. The general scheme of English 'opera' at this time was modelled on the French *comédie-ballet,* the main principle being that each act of a spoken play should conclude with a musical interlude. We can trace this back to the Italian comedies of the early Renaissance, with *intermedi* of music and dancing, with very elaborate scenery, between the acts. The English, like the French, were most unwilling to accept the idea of a play that was entirely set to music. The result is that the play is acted by one company, and the music performed by another; the chief actors never sing at all. In fact, English opera of the seventeenth century, as far as the public theatre was concerned, was never anything more than a romantic play with a great deal of incidental music. Shadwell, however, went further than Molière, for instead of confining the music to the ends of the acts, he interspersed it elsewhere. Thus the first act begins with the entrance of Psyche and two attendants; after a little talking, music is heard, and Pan enters with a chorus to crown Psyche with flowers, which gives an opportunity for songs and dances. Act II begins with a long ceremony in the temple of Apollo, all set to music. There is a very beautiful effect in Act IV; Psyche is about to drown herself in a river, when the god of the river rises to music, attended by nymphs, who tell her to bear her sufferings with patience, and promise her immortality hereafter. In Molière's play the river-god is seen reclining on his urn all through the act, and his address to Psyche is spoken; Shadwell's treatment of the entry is much more picturesque and Locke's music has a remarkable beauty

153

and solemnity. The fact that the river-god and nymphs all sing raises them at once to a higher plane.

A collection of music to *Macbeth* was published in 1750, edited by Dr Boyce and ascribed to Locke. It was often performed at concerts in the eighteenth century, and even in the nineteenth it was fairly well known. Its real authorship is uncertain; it is not likely to be the work of Locke at all. Some authorities supposed it to be a youthful effort of Purcell; others put forward Leveridge as the composer. It is crude and ungainly, but it has a certain sense of stage effect and it also has continuity, which gives it some value as a step towards English operatic writing. The words set are not Shakespeare's, but are the interpolations from Middleton's play, *The Witch*.

To about the same date belongs Locke's music for *The Tempest*, not much of which has survived; the most interesting number is an instrumental interlude evidently meant to represent a storm.

All these plays with music were parodied at the time by Thomas Duffett, who may be regarded as the creator of the English pantomime, which is really a bastard descendant of the English opera. In his skit on *Macbeth* 'Three Witches fly over the Pit riding upon Beesomes ... *Heccate* descends over the Stage in a Glorious Charriott adorn'd with Pictures of Hell and Devils, and made of a large Wicker Basket.' Two spirits enter with burning brandy, which they drink. *Psyche* was more elaborately parodied, and in view of modern pantomime it is amusing to note that the two princes were acted by women, and Psyche herself – here called None-so-fair, or Nonsey for short – by Joe Haines, the famous low comedian.

Another skit on English opera was *The Rehearsal,* by the Duke of Buckingham, first printed in 1672. The dance of soldiers, which caused so much trouble, was probably an allusion to *The History of Sir Francis Drake,* for Locke often wrote pantomimic dances of a grotesque type with sudden pauses and changes of *tempo*; Mr Bayes (i.e. D'Avenant) remarks to the soldiers:

'Udzookers, you dance worse than the Angels in *Harry the Eight,* or the fat spirits in *The Tempest,* egad.'

154

The battle, represented by two men only, is an allusion to *The Siege of Rhodes*. The two combatants appear in armour, with drawn swords, and a scarlet ribbon at their wrists, each holding a lute in his hand.

I make 'em Sir, play the battel in *Recitativo*. And here's the conceipt. Just at the very same instant that one sings, the other, Sir, recovers you his sword, and puts himself in a warlike posture; so that you have at once your ear entertain'd with Music, and good Language, and your eye satisfied with the garb, and accoutrements of War.

The performance of *The Tempest* in 1674 at Dorset Garden Theatre was apparently the first at which the orchestra was placed in what is now its normal position. Hitherto it had always been in a gallery over the stage, unless it was associated with devils below, in which case the acoustics were unsatisfactory, as Pepys tells us. The transfer allowed for a much larger orchestra (24 strings, with harpsichord and theorbos), and also established the presence of an orchestra as a recognized convention; in the earlier theatre the instrumentalists had always been invisible, unless they had to come on to the stage as actors to play a serenade, or something of that sort. The musicians had been hidden in the first Italian operas, too, as we have already seen.

Shakespeare had himself laid down the principle that music, when not brought on to the stage in the way mentioned just now, was generally to be associated with supernatural characters and happenings. Ariel sings because he is a spirit; the function of music was to open the door to the realm of mystery. Purcell's famous music to *The Tempest* was composed for a much later performance.

Some ten years later Dryden conceived the idea of writing the libretto for an English opera on a plan of his own. He tells us about it in the preface to *Albion and Albanius,* which was one of the unluckiest attempts at opera ever put on the English stage. Dryden was as ready to theorize about opera as Wagner himself, and his observations on English opera are extremely interesting. He begins by explaining what an opera is:

An *Opera* is a Poetical Tale, or Fiction, represented by Vocal and Instrumental Musick, adorn'd with Scenes, Machines and Dancing.

The suppos'd Persons of this Musical *Drama*, are generally Supernatural, as Gods, and Goddesses, and Heroes, which at least are descended from them, and are in due time to be adopted into their number.

He will also allow 'meaner persons' to be introduced if it can be managed gracefully, and if they can be connected with the 'golden age':

and therefore Shepherds might reasonably be admitted, as of all Callings, the most innocent, the most happy, and also by reason of the spare Time they had, in their almost idle Employment, had most leisure to make Verses, and to be in Love, without somewhat of which Passion, no *Opera* can possibly subsist.

Albion and Albanius had originally been intended to be nothing more than a short prologue in the traditional French style to the main drama. This was to be

a Tragedy mix'd with Opera; or a *Drama* written in blank verse, adorn'd with scenes, Machines, songs and dances: So that the Fable of it is all spoken and acted by the best of the Comedians; the other part of the Entertainment to be perform'd by the same Singers and Dancers, who are introduced in this present opera [i.e. *Albion and Albanius* in its extended form]. It cannot properly be called a Play, because the Action of it is supposed to be conducted sometimes by supernatural Means, or Magick; nor an *Opera*, because the Story of it is not sung.

For some unknown reason the performance of the main drama was postponed, and the prologue was expanded into three acts. The music was composed by Louis Grabu, a Frenchman who had managed to make himself a favourite at court. He evidently knew little English, and he made a sad hash of Dryden's words.

The story, if one can call it so, would have done well enough for a prologue in the style of Lully, as the characters were all either classical divinities or allergorical figures; but it could not make a whole opera, even with better music than Grabu's. It is interesting to note that Dryden printed the list of characters (which is very large) in the order of their appearance, a practice that was then unusual, and did not reappear, I believe, until it was revived on the programmes of the Stage Society about 1900.

156

The first scene is a street of palaces leading to the Royal Exchange, with equestrian statues of Charles I and Charles II. Augusta (London) and Thamesis are lying on couches in dejected postures; Mercury descends in a chariot drawn by ravens, reproves Augusta for her disloyalty and promises to restore Albion (i.e. Charles II) to her. Democracy and Puritanism enter, but are dispatched to the nether regions by General Monk. Thamesis calls for a dance of watermen; Juno appears in a machine drawn by peacocks, Iris comes over from Holland 'on a very large machine' to announce that Albion has had a safe crossing. The act ends with the entrance of Albion and Albanius (James) in procession.

This act is complete in itself as a prologue. The second and third act symbolize the Popish Plot and the Rye House Plot. At the end Albion invokes Proteus, who after changing himself into a lion, a crocodile and a dragon, prophesies the future. Venus rises from the sea attended by Graces, Loves and Heroes escorting Albanius; Apollo descends from heaven attended 'by abundance of Angels and Cherubims', and carries Albion up with him (death of Charles II). The opera ends with a view of Windsor Castle and a procession of Knights of the Garter; Fame rises on a pedestal and sings the praises of Albion.

Many of the things in this opera seem to foreshadow Wagner, such as the birds, the dragon and the rainbow (Iris). But Wagner's gods do at least behave like human beings, whereas Dryden's do nothing but explain who they are; it is the old tradition of the Jacobean masque. All that can be said is that it was a good thing that all this allegorical nonsense was foisted on to the incompetent Monsieur Grabu, and that the real drama was left for Purcell to set some years later.

The next attempt at opera called itself a masque, but was in fact a genuine opera – the first real opera ever produced in England since *The Siege of Rhodes*. The date of it is uncertain, but it was probably about 1685 that John Blow (1648–1708) composed his *Venus and Adonis*, a little opera in three acts for the private entertainment of the king. The part of Venus was sung by Mrs Mary Davis, mistress of the King, and that of Cupid by her daughter, on whom her royal father had conferred the title of Lady Mary Tudor. She was born in 1673, so that she might have been about twelve or less when she sang the part; and she must have been a very accomplished little musician.

Everything about *Venus and Adonis* is so small that one could imagine it better suited to a puppet theatre than to performance by living people; it is far too intimate and delicate for an ordinary opera house. But there is no mistake about the poignancy of its emotion, and it has some delightfully humorous moments as well; in fact its most striking characteristic is the way in which it quite suddenly passes from frivolity to tragedy. There can be no doubt that it served as the model for Purcell's *Dido and Aeneas*.

Henry Purcell (1658–1695) had been brought up to be a church musician, but he had begun his connexion with the theatre in 1680, when he wrote incidental music for Lee's *Theodosius*, mostly scenes of religious ceremony. For the next few years he had few opportunities of showing what he could do, as Grabu was all-powerful in the fashionable world of music. But about 1689 – that date is not absolutely certain – Josias Priest, a teacher of dancing who acted as ballet master at the theatres and was also proprietor of a school for young ladies in Chelsea, invited Purcell to compose a short opera for the pupils to perform. It is possible that Purcell may have been the regular music-master at the school, but we have absolutely no information about the performance. The words of the little opera were written by Nahum Tate, better known as the author (with Nicholas Brady) of a metrical version of the Psalter. Tate was at that time Poet Laureate. He seems to have drawn his materials from a play which he had written in 1678 called *Brutus of Alba*; it is the story of Dido and Aeneas under different names, but Brutus was supposed to be a descendant of Aeneas, who came to England and built a city which he called New Troy, now London. A study of this play explains some of the obscurities in *Dido and Aeneas*; certain things had to be left out as unsuitable for a girls' school, and an important male character had to be suppressed, probably for want of anyone to act him.

Dido and Aeneas had presumably one performance at the school, and in 1700 it was inserted as a masque into a performance of *Measure for Measure*; after that it was given only in a much mutilated concert arrangement during the eighteenth century. It was not put on the stage again until the bi-centenary of Purcell's death in 1895, when it was acted at the Royal College of Music, since when it has had a great many performances, mostly by amateurs. Except for a few perform-ances at Sadler's Wells, our professional opera companies have ignored it; but it has been performed in Germany (Münster and Stuttgart), at Vienna, Paris, Florence Rome and Budapest, as well as in many places in America.

Purcell tells the story of Dido in the simplest way, but for a seventeenth-century audience witches were indispensable (though we may wonder whether Mr Priest's young ladies flew on besoms), so they are introduced to supply a new motive for the departure of Aeneas. In the first scene we see Dido brooding over her sorrows; she is comforted by Belinda and the chorus. Aeneas enters and is received by Dido; the whole court leave for a hunting party. The second scene shows the witches' cave. The Sorceress plans the destruction of Dido, apparently out of pure class-hatred, and the witches prepare a charm. A false spirit is to be sent to meet Aeneas, as a sup-posed messenger from the gods, to tell him that he must leave Carthage at once. The hunting party occupies the third scene; Dido and Aeneas are resting after Aeneas has slain a boar. A thunderstorm suddenly comes on, and as all prepare to depart in haste, the spirit appears and bids Aeneas forsake Dido for ever; the scene ends with his despair. The fourth scene is laid at the harbour, where sailors and women are carousing; after this very English picture of seaport life, Dido enters to make a last effort to dissuade Aeneas from departing. After a very moving dialogue he tears himself away; the chorus gravely comment on the situation, and the opera ends with the suicide of Dido on her funeral pyre.

Dido and Aeneas, if performed without intervals, as is desir-able, lasts little over an hour, but its emotional range is so wide that one can hardly believe the opera to be so short. Purcell's musical style is his own; it is derived partly from Blow, his teacher, partly from the Italian cantata style of Monteverdi's day. The dances owe something to Lully, but much more to Locke and the old English tradition of the masques. They are a very important part of the opera, and, indeed, the whole opera gains by being treated rather in the manner of a ballet, as was done with great success by Kurt Jooss for the German production at Münster in 1926.

Having been composed for a school, *Dido and Aeneas* is not well suited to a large theatre, and it will not bear adapting to modern methods such as the orchestration of the recitatives and the addition of wind instruments; such attempts to bring it up to date simply destroy its very carefully designed proportions. When given according to the original score, it is astonishing what startling effects Purcell can obtain with the barest resources.

We may well imagine that among the guests invited to that school 'speech-day' in Chelsea was the famous actor, Betterton, with whom Priest had often collaborated. At any rate his next theatrical venture was *Dioclesian* (1690), for which he engaged Purcell to compose a large quantity of music. *Dioclesian,* however, cannot be classed as an opera, any more than *The Tempest* and *The Indian Queen,* for both of which Purcell wrote music of great interest. The result of all these plays with music seems to have been the conversion of Dryden to a better appreciation of Purcell, and in 1691 they collaborated over *King Arthur,* the drama to which *Albion and Albanius* had been intended to form a prologue.

Musicians are generally inclined to consider *The Fairy Queen* a better work than *King Arthur*; there is a larger amount of music in it, and certainly more single numbers of pure musical beauty. But *King Arthur* stands by itself as the joint creation of a great poet and dramatist with a great musician, working in real collaboration; and it is a serious effort to solve the artistic problem of English opera. This cannot be said of any other so-called operas of Purcell, for they were all adaptations of plays originally intended to be acted without any great amount of music.

Dryden started from the principle that ordinary mortals in a drama must speak and not sing; but in order to make this play as much of an opera as possible he introduced several supernatural characters, for whom music was the natural language. He must have learned something from Shadwell too, for he is very skilful at bringing in music at all sorts of places, in such a way that it becomes integral to the drama.

The plot of *King Arthur* is excessively patriotic, so much so, indeed, that it might well move a modern audience to laughter at times; but Purcell's music is still so magnificent that whenever it begins we are obliged to surrender to its beauty. King Arthur, it is well to say at the outset, has nothing whatever to do with Glastonbury and the Round Table; he is a Christian King of Britain fighting against Oswald, the Saxon King of Kent, who has made war on him because he is his rival for the hand of Emmeline, the blind daughter of Conon, Duke of Cornwall.

The first act introduces the characters, and the great musical moment is the scene in which Oswald propitiates the heathen gods Woden, Thor and Freya with a human sacrifice. He has two spirits at his command, Grimbald, 'a fierce, earthly spirit', and Philidel, 'an airy spirit'. After the sacrifice a battle takes place in which the Britons are victorious, the act ending with the well-known chorus, 'Come, if you dare'.

In Act II Philidel goes over to the side of Arthur at the behest of the enchanter Merlin. Arthur and his soldiers enter, led by Grimbald, disguised as a shepherd, whose object is to mislead them into bogs and marshes; Philidel rescues them and brings them to safety. This is all set to music, with two opposing choruses of spirits. The next scene is taken up with Emmeline and her blindness; Oswald enters and Emmeline is carried off by his men. The music to Act III has been to some extent lost, which is a pity, as the situations would have called for Purcell at his best. Merlin restores sight to Emmeline, but she cannot yet escape from the spells of the rival enchanter, Osmond, who is in the service of Oswald. Osmond, having drugged his master, makes violent love to the princess, and in order to encourage her shows her a land covered with ice and snow in which the inhabitants are warmed to love by the arts of Cupid.

Act IV shows us an enchanted wood through which Arthur is trying to find his way to Emmeline; at every turn he is beset by sirens and nymphs who try to distract him from his purpose. Emmeline appears in a tree-trunk, but turns out to be Grimbald in another disguise. Finally in Act V, Arthur and Oswald fight a single combat, each supported by his attendant wizard; Oswald is, of course, defeated, and the play ends with the surrender of the Saxons and the marriage of Arthur and Emmeline. Merlin waves his wand, and spirits perform a masque in honour of St George and the Order of the Garter.

One cannot help being struck by the number of episodes in this opera which suggest Wagner – the hero accosted, like Siegfried, by the sirens in the river, the slow entrance of the Frost Genius, like the evocation of Erda, the duel with the attendant enchanters, like the fight between Hunding and Siegmund in *The Valkyrie*, to say nothing of the heathen sacrifices in the first act.

King Arthur is a great English classic of the stage, and it ought certainly to be revived from time to time, all the more as it offers great opportunities for actors and dancers as well as for singers, such as the Old Vic could easily supply in conjunction with Sadler's Wells. The same sort of cooperation would be needed for *The Fairy Queen* (1692 and 1693), which is an adaptation of *A Midsummer Night's Dream* on similar lines, but confining the music entirely to the ends of the acts. Devout admirers of Shakespeare are sometimes gravely shocked at the idea of sacrificing a word of the original play for the sake of Purcell's music, for it has to be admitted that Purcell did not set a single line of Shakespeare in this opera. It is Shakespeare seen through Restoration eyes, and when we remember Mr Pepys's judgement on *A Midsummer Night's Dream* – 'the most insipid, ridiculous play that I ever saw in my life' – we can hardly wonder that it was considered only fit to make an opera libretto.

The attitude which we of today may reasonably take can be illustrated by what we see in a picture-gallery. Two artists have painted much the same sort of picture; one calls it 'The Flight into Egypt', the other 'Landscape with figures', and the spectator may choose for himself whether he is more interested in the figures or in the landscape. I cannot think it a sacrilege to act a mutilated version of Shakespeare in order that we may see Purcell's opera on the stage. Purcell's music was written for the stage, and it is never effective without it, though attempts have been made to turn it into a cantata with words about entirely different subjects. Nor is it possible to utilize Purcell for an orthodox performance of the play. The only thing to do is to restore, as far as possible, the actual wording of Shakespeare in place of the anonymous adapter's revisions, and to cut down the play ruthlessly to make time for Purcell's music. The famous passages of pure poetry must all go, and so must the complete performance of *Pyramus and Thisbe*; we must accept what Purcell has to give us in lieu of them. If *A Midsummer Night's Dream* was a play rarely acted or even read, then we might hesitate; but today it is the best-known play of Shakespeare; every modern child has acted in it at school or has been taken to see it. One can see a hundred performances of the play for one of the opera, and the sacrifice of one performance out of a hundred is no very great price to pay for the fascinating experience of *The Fairy Queen*.

CHAPTER ELEVEN

OPERA IN ENGLAND – HANDEL – 'THE BEGGAR'S
OPERA' – BALFE AND WALLACE – COVENT GARDEN
AND SADLER'S WELLS

THE untimely death of Purcell in 1695 brought English opera to an end, at least as far as Purcell's type of opera was concerned, although *King Arthur* had many revivals, sometimes with additional music by later composers; there was even a performance as late as 1842. After that it does not seem to have been put on the stage (although the music was often sung at concerts) until the Cambridge revival of 1928. During Purcell's lifetime the fashion for Italian music, and especially for Italian singing, was gradually gaining ground, but the Italian singers who came over appeared only at concerts until 1703, when 'interludes and mimical entertainments of singing and dancing' were performed in Italian. These *intermezzi* were probably comic scenes for two characters from the operas of Scarlatti and others; they might easily have formed part of a concert. Purcell had already written several dramatic duets of the same sort for various plays. In 1706 Thomas Clayton, a musician of no particular ability, who had travelled in Italy, put on the stage an opera called *Arsinoe*; the words were translated from an Italian libretto of 1676. The music was described on the title-page of the score as 'compos'd by Mr Tho. Clayton', but it was alleged by Hawkins in his *History of Music* that Clayton merely adapted Italian airs that he had collected in Italy. The singers were all English, and the opera had a fair success. It was followed by *Camilla*, an opera by Marcantonio Buononcini (Naples, 1696) in a translation by Owen Mac-Swiney. In 1706 Addison, whom one would not have suspected of operatic interests, judging by his sneers at the opera in *The Spectator*, wrote a libretto on the subject of Henry II and Fair Rosamond, which was set to music by Clayton. *Rosamond* was a complete failure, and Burney, who could never forgive

Addison his disrespect to Handel, makes great fun of this opera, in which 'the King's approach to the bower of bliss is always announced by a loud concert of military instruments'. It is curious to note that Addison follows the Italian custom of introducing two comic characters into his serious opera.

So far the Italian operas had been given in English, but when Nicolini (Niccolo Grimaldi), the great Italian *castrato*, came to England in 1708, the practice began of singing them partly in English and partly in Italian, to suit the nationality of the singers taking part. This began with *Pyrrhus and Demetrius,* an adaptation of an opera by Alessandro Scarlatti. By this time the opera was established in Vanbrugh's new theatre in the Haymarket, known after Queen Anne's death as the King's Theatre; it remained the chief home of opera in London until it was burned down in 1789, and its successor on the same site continued the tradition (under the name of Her Majesty's Theatre, after the accession of Queen Victoria) for another hundred years. It was burned again in 1867 and rebuilt; it was finally pulled down in 1891.

The first opera performed entirely in Italian was *Almahide* (1710); it is not known who was the composer, and very probably it was a *pasticcio* made up from songs by various composers. This method of compiling Italian operas became very common in England later on, and set a bad example for the English operas of the century.

Dr Burney's remarks on the establishment of Italian opera in England are interesting, because they state a point of view which many people hold today.

> Music is a Manufacture in Italy, that feeds and enriches a large portion of the people; and it is no more disgraceful to a mercantile country to import it, than wine, tea, or any other production of remote parts of the world. . . .
>
> The vocal Music of Italy can only be heard in perfection when sung to its own language and by its own natives, who give both the language and Music their true accents and expressions. There is as much reason for wishing to hear Italian Music performed in this genuine manner, as for the lovers of painting to prefer an original picture of Raphael to a copy.

It was in this same year, 1710, that Handel (1685–1759) arrived in England for the first time. His opera *Rinaldo* was

165

performed the following year, and for the next thirty years he continued to produce Italian operas for London. There is no need to pursue his career in detail; the story of his rivalry with Giovanni Buononcini (brother of the composer of *Camilla*), his misadventures with singers and his financial embarrassments belong to his own biography. His last opera, *Deidamia,* came out in 1741, and after that he devoted himself solely to oratorio.

During the last twenty years considerable efforts have been made, especially in Germany, to resuscitate Handel's operas and to convince the world that he was a great dramatic composer. There can be little doubt that opera was the form of music which Handel himself preferred, else why should he have continued writing operas for so many years in the face of perpetual opposition and financial disaster? The money which he made out of his operas was derived far more from the sale of printed copies than from receipts in the theatre. It is very difficult to form an honest opinion on Handel's operas at the present day. About Handel's individual genius there is, of course, no question, and every one of the operas gives examples of it. In single airs and recitatives, sometimes in whole scenes, his dramatic insight and his force of expression are very striking. But it is difficult to pick out a single opera in which he shows a consistent and continuous sense of drama, and sometimes his personages are made to change character quite unaccountably, merely because the poet has given them songs which have tempted Handel to compose lovely music without any regard for the stage situation.

The plain fact is that Handel's audiences did not want real drama; they wanted fine singing. Burney analyses every one of the operas, but he never even comes near telling us what they are about. He merely gives us a list of the songs, assigning each not to the character represented but to the singer who sang it. If the songs were dramatic in character, so much the better; but this was always placed to the credit of the individual singer and had no bearing on the drama as a whole – or rather, the drama as a whole had no interest for the majority of the connoisseurs. If Handel's operas are to be revived today solely for the connoisseurs of singing, a new race of singers will have to be bred up, for modern singers are ill at ease in Handel.

Still, a Handel opera offers interesting problems to the modern producer and decorator, and if a start could once be made, it is conceivable that Handel operas in English might achieve a certain success.

Handel's retirement made no great difference to the Italian opera seasons. They were carried on by a succession of syndicates, and although a good deal of money was thrown away, new syndicates were always willing to face the risks. It is noteworthy, however, that after Handel's death comic opera begins to make more and more frequent appearances in the Italian season. Italian the season always remained; Dr Burney takes us as far as the early operas of Cherubini, but throughout the century French opera seems to have been unknown in this country.

A few attempts were made in the early years of the century to revive English opera; even Locke's *Psyche* was given a chance, but in view of the aristocratic preference for Italian opera, there could be no hope for English opera of a serious type. It was the same in all the other countries, as we have seen in the previous chapters; serious opera, either Italian or French, for the court and the aristocracy, comic opera in the native language for 'the people'. The people, it may be said, were also largely recruited from the aristocracy.

A new impulse was given to English comic opera by the production of *The Beggar's Opera* in 1728. The words were by Gay, the music arranged by Dr Pepusch from all kinds of popular tunes. It was not the first opera made up from popular tunes, for Durfey's *Wonder in the Sun* (1706) had songs which were 'all set to ballad tunes of a true English growth', according to Burney. *The Beggar's Opera* has sometimes been described as a parody of the Handelian opera, but there are very few allusions to the Italian opera in it, although a favourite march of Handel's is included. Nor is it true to say that the tunes of *The Beggar's Opera* are all English folk-songs; many are Scottish and Irish, a few French, Italian and Portuguese, besides known songs by Purcell and his contemporaries. It would be more accurate to say that many of these tunes have been accepted as folk-songs owing to the permanent popularity of the opera. It had many revivals in the eighteenth century, and was well known in the earlier part of the nineteenth. Victorian taste required it to be a good deal bowdlerized, and towards the end of the century it was considered impossible. In June, 1920, a new version, in which the tunes were reharmonized by Frederic Austin, was brought out at the Lyric Theatre, Hammersmith, with brilliantly clever scenery and costumes by Lovat Fraser; it ran continuously until the end of 1923. The original success of this work was due largely to the topical satire of the play, and the sequel, *Polly*, was forbidden. *Polly* was revived after the success of the Hammersmith enterprise; but it had only a short run. The latest version so far is that of Benjamin Britten (Cambridge, 1948), which treats the old tunes with completely modern harmony and brilliant orchestral virtuosity.

The success of the first performance of *The Beggar's Opera* produced a never-ending succession of 'ballad operas', as they were called, and it is generally held that the importation of these into Germany was the origin of the German *Singspiel* or comic opera with spoken dialogue and songs. The ballad operas enjoyed great popularity in their day, and many of the songs in them became great favourites, to be found in all popular anthologies right down to the present day. Some of them were traditional ballad tunes, others were composed for the operas; but not a single one of these operas has passed into the permanent repertory, though occasional attempts at revival have been made. Composers like Arne and Dibdin wrote for them, but they did not take much trouble over them, and in most of the ballad operas the music was pieced together from various sources, often from popular foreign operas. As time went on the ensemble became an attraction, and that had to be written by some local composer; but for the most part these ensembles are rather helpless affairs, though some of them obtained long popularity in the form of glees.

The historical importance of the ballad operas lies in the fact that they gradually created a peculiarly English style of popular tune, not folk-song, but definitely urban and theatrical; it persisted all through the nineteenth century and is not yet extinct despite the rival attractions of American and Austrian trivialities. There are plenty of old ballad operas which if played through today at once provoke the remark, 'Why, it's almost like Sullivan!'

In the year of Gluck's *Orfeo*, 1762, a serious attempt at English opera was made by Arne (1710-78), who translated Metastasio's *Artaxerxes* and set it to music in the Italian style with recitatives and florid airs; it was admired in its day, but had no successors. Arne, like many English composers, was a generation behind his time; the sort of opera that he wanted to write was already dying out everywhere. Early in the nineteenth century Bishop (1786-1855) showed some ability for operatic composition; he has even been called the English Rossini. But the commercial outlook of managers made anything like serious opera impossible for him; a great deal of his time was spent in adapting foreign operas, which meant cutting them about and interpolating numbers by other composers. It seemed to be taken for granted that an English opera must be some sort of a *pasticcio*.

The romantic novel was very much an English product, and it was only natural that England should cultivate the romantic opera; but the music was always regarded as a subsidiary matter, and this is evident from the fact that when Weber was commissioned to compose *Oberon* for Covent Garden in 1826, the words of the songs were sent to him at Dresden one after another, without any of the connecting dialogue, so that Weber had no idea of how they fitted into the drama and complained to Planché, the author, who seemed much surprised.

The success of Weber's and Marschner's romantic operas in London led to visits from German companies; *Fidelio* was such a success when interpreted by Mme Schröder-Devrient in 1832 that it was repeated in English by Malibran with even greater success the following year.

About this time several English operas were produced which had considerable success, though few of them are remembered now. The first was *The Mountain Sylph* (1834), by John Barnett, who was a first cousin of Meyerbeer. The scene is laid in Scotland.

Aeolia, a mountain sylph, having encountered Donald, a young Scotsman betrothed to Jessie, falls in love with the handsome mortal, and to gain him herself, so fascinates him that at the very moment of being united to his bride, he escapes with the fairy, leaving all the wedding guests in consternation, with the exception of the simple-minded

Christie, his unsuccessful rival, who now has a chance of obtaining Jessie's hand.

In a forest glade, whither they had retired, the sylph coquettishly evades Donald, who urges his suit with ardour; whereupon Hela, the wizard of the glen – who secretly hates Donald, and has planned both revenge on him and the sylph's destruction – offers him a magic scarf, by entwining which round the fairy she will be at his mercy. Donald, unaware of the foul design of the sorcerer, casts it around her; immediately her wings drop off, she falls dying to earth, is seized by the fiend Ashtaroth and sinks into the Salamandrine Caverns, leaving Donald in despair and Hela triumphant. Then Etheria, Queen of the Sylphs, descending, gives to Donald a magic rose, by which he penetrates into the burning regions, delivers the captive sylph, and re-ascends with her to the earth, where their love is blessed by Etheria, as is also the union of Christie and Jessie.

This concise summary, taken from the vocal score, gives a sufficient account of the plot, and leads us naturally to expect that the music will be an imitation of Weber, more often of the mellifluous Marschner, with a little Scotch thrown in. The libretto by J. J. Thackeray is ludicrously awkward and the composer has to repeat words over and over again to spin out his arias and his interminable ensembles and finales. The commonplace character of the themes could be forgiven if they had any sort of popular attractiveness, but the construction is generally very amateurish and the music is always coming to a dead stop when it ought to go on.

In the following year, 1835, Michael William Balfe (1808–70) began his career as a composer of English operas with *The Siege of Rochelle*, produced at Drury Lane, where there were many seasons of opera in English under various managements. Balfe had had some experience as a singer in Italy, and had even composed a few Italian operas; one was written in twenty days, and we need not be surprised, for it was a period when opera was not taken too seriously. No British composer has ever enjoyed so much success, and success all over Europe, as Balfe; he wrote over thirty operas, but only one of them is ever heard now – *The Bohemian Girl* (1843).

The Bohemian Girl and *Maritana* (1845), by another Irishman, W. V. Wallace (1812–65), have become such national classics that they seem to be beyond criticism. The English

170

operas of this period have become a byword for absurdity, mainly owing to their librettos, especially those written by Alfred Bunn and Edward Fitzball. They read as if they were translations, and the reason is that they were imitations of foreign styles. *The Siege of Rochelle* is an obvious imitation of Auber; it has all the typical features that one expects to find in a French *opéra-comique* – the long, chattering song for the comic servant, here in praise of England, just as its prototypes sang the delights of Paris, and before that, of Naples; the *couplets*, i.e. songs in two or three stanzas, the semi-military song of the heroic young man, and the ensembles in block harmony, with the finale in three-four time, getting faster and faster and louder and louder. The English librettists knew exactly what was wanted, but they did not take much trouble about their versification. Probably no one cared in those days if the tunes made nonsense of the words because the poet had carried the sense on from one line to the next without allowing for the inevitable stop at the ends of the musical phrases.

We do wrong at the present day to apply 'grand opera' standards to these romantic operas that were descended from comic operas and not from *opera seria*. The comic element, which comes out very clearly in the spoken dialogue, was the foundation; it is the heroic element which is episodical, for in these operas even heroes are allowed to have a sense of humour, at any rate when talking. Their songs seem absurd, because the function of music here is to illustrate violent emotion, and just the sort of violent emotion which the ordinary Englishman would restrain. And our language is ill-suited to such expression, as one soon finds out if one tries to write English words for the rapturous airs of Rossini. The result is that any English words are apt to sound ludicrous set to such conventionally rapturous music, all the more so after we have become acquainted with the character in the normal humorous mood of common speech. If we find *Maritana* and *The Bohemian Girl* laughable on the modern stage, no great harm is done; as a matter of fact, an ordinary English audience is always held in tense silence, however old-fashioned the music may be, if the singer has a good voice and sings with conviction. And all tenors sing with conviction, for they are firmly convinced that their own voices are all that matters.

171

The most prosperous period of English romantic opera was between 1856 and 1864, when Louisa Pyne, a distinguished soprano, and William Harrison, a tenor, formed a partnership to manage what was called on their printed librettos 'The Royal English Opera'. It was heartily supported by the Prince Consort, and there were even hopes that he would be able to obtain a parliamentary subsidy for it; but his death in 1861 put an end to that. In 1875 Carl Rosa, a violinist from Hamburg, founded the company which still bears his name, though he died in 1889. Rosa was a man of great courage and enterprise; he produced *The Flying Dutchman* in English in 1876 and *Rienzi* in 1879, besides giving the first English performance of *Carmen* (1879). And the Carl Rosa company by no means limited itself to foreign operas; it achieved honour, if not success, in the production of several new works by native composers such as Goring Thomas, Cowen, Mackenzie and Stanford. These men represented a new generation and a new outlook on music and on opera. The days of the 'Poet Bunn' were at an end, and English opera was now to be taken seriously. The only trouble was that none of these composers had very much sense of the stage, and the same can be said of their librettists. Goring Thomas, who died young, had considerable charm of melody in a very French style, but his operas are too slight for modern taste. The others were all more at home in the concert-room than in the theatre, and their operas suffered from too much academic restraint.

Cowen and Mackenzie soon gave up the attempt; Stanford (1852–1924), with a more than Handelian courage, continued writing operas to the end of his life, though hardly any of them attained popularity. The Carl Rosa Company found itself obliged to play for safety, and reverted generally to the well-known favourites. Augustus Harris, who had been for some years associated with Rosa, began in 1887 to organize international Italian opera, which had struggled along under various managements all through the century. Harris's management of Covent Garden from 1888 to 1896, the year of his death, was exceptionally brilliant, and the syndicate which succeeded him maintained an equally high standard for several years. English composers, however, did not receive much encouragement, except for the works of Isidore de Lara (real name Cohen, 1858–1935), which were all in French and made the voluptuosities of Massenet seem puritanical by comparison.

One work of Stanford's was produced in English, *Much Ado About Nothing* (1901), but it was withdrawn after two performances, much to the composer's indignation. Outside Covent Garden the only hope for a British composer was to find a manager who would put his work on for a run, which was a very risky undertaking. None the less, Stanford had a considerable success with his Irish comic opera *Shamus O'Brien* (1896); it continues the old English tradition of opera with spoken dialogue, and comedy as the main feature with romantic episodes. It was alleged that it gave great offence to Queen Victoria because it made fun of the English army in Ireland; sympathy with the Ireland of 1798 was considered suspicious in those days. *The Travelling Companion* (Bristol, 1926) has had several performances at Sadler's Wells.

An earlier attempt had been made to produce grand opera for a run with Sullivan's (1842–1900) *Ivanhoe* (1891); it reached the remarkable figure of one hundred and sixty nights, but it has very seldom been performed since. The libretto, by Julian Sturgis, has considerable distinction – too much, perhaps, for the recitatives in Tennysonian blank verse often become tedious; there is too much 'literature' about them for the amount of information that they convey. Sullivan, always anxious to give his voices every chance and never to overload them with orchestration, set them mostly in a far too leisurely style. The opera contains many attractive songs, which in their day were very popular concert numbers; in the opera they stand out rather too conspicuously as such, all the more since Sullivan, like Mozart, was careful to provide every singer with at least one opportunity of taking the stage in the grand manner. Another reason why opera companies are shy of reviving *Ivanhoe* is that it calls for pageantry on the grand scale and has three separate scenes in each act; the audiences of those days never seemed to mind sitting through a large number of intervals.

During the first years of the new century it looked as if interest in opera was rapidly increasing in London, and gradually the influence of New York began to make itself felt there as well. The Metropolitan Opera House of New York had been opened in 1883; it was burned ten years later, but rebuilt, and soon quite eclipsed Covent Garden in the splendour of its international performances. American singers, many of whom were artists of supreme excellence, appeared in London and at all the important Continental opera houses, and gradually a certain 'star standard' established itself for three theatres, the Metropolitan, Covent Garden, and Monte Carlo. This had a not altogether fortunate effect on English opera-singing, for whereas the French, German and Italian singers all normally appeared in routine opera in their own countries, the English and the Americans had no such advantages. There was no permanent opera in English in any country; the travelling companies in the United States were mostly German or Italian, and the 'heavyweight' singers of British nationality sometimes thought themselves too grand for the Carl Rosa or for the Moody-Manners Company, which at this time was doing very enterprising work in the provinces. It became the ambition of every English opera singer to appear at Covent Garden, and there were plenty of opportunities in minor parts, sometimes even in very important ones, as long as the singer was prepared to tackle them in Italian, German or French. The acknowledged queen of this international group was an Australian, who sang under the name of Melba, and who will go down to posterity as one of the most famous singers of the world; she appears never to have sung opera in her native language in her life.

Two new stars appeared on the operatic horizon in 1909, when Thomas Beecham conducted performances of *The Wreckers,* an English opera by Ethel Smyth (1858–1944). It was by no means her first opera; two previous works had been produced in Germany, and *The Wreckers,* written to a French libretto, had had its first production in German at Leipzig in 1906. The only hope for English composers at that time was to write their operas in some foreign language, for even if they were put on at Covent Garden with the help of a substantial guarantee, English was not looked upon with favour.

Beecham's policy for the moment was to perform the operas which interested him, out-of-the-way works rather than established favourites. He gave a short season in February,

1910, at Covent Garden, opening with Strauss's *Elektra*; the real novelty of the season was *The Village Romeo and Juliet* by Frederick Delius (1862–1934), first brought out in German at Berlin in 1907. It was the beginning of a long campaign in favour of Delius as a composer, and the enthusiastic recognition accorded to Delius shortly before his death was almost entirely due to the energies of Beecham. *The Wreckers* and *Ivanhoe* were both revived at this season.

The outbreak of war in 1914 put an end to the international summer season at Covent Garden, which was utilized by the Government to store the furniture of various hotels taken over for Government offices. It was entirely owing to the enthusiasm of Beecham that opera was carried on at all during the four years of the war; and as most foreigners had left the country, the operas had to be in English. The result of this was that the public began to become much more 'opera-conscious' than it had ever been before, and it also got into the habit of regarding English as a natural language for opera. The result was the formation in 1922 of the British National Opera Company, which for some years gave excellent performances in the provinces, with a higher standard of orchestral playing than had generally been observed.

After the war was over Covent Garden started the international season again in 1919. Beecham was naturally the chief director, and he followed up the international season with an English season in November and December of the same year, and another English season from February to April. But the winter season of 1920 was left to the Carl Rosa, and in 1921 there was no opera at Covent Garden of any kind.

Meanwhile, opera in English had been going on for years in a very humble way at the Old Vic in Waterloo Road. Miss Emma Cons, a philanthropist, had taken over the theatre in 1880; up till then it had had a rather lurid reputation, but Miss Cons transformed it into a cheap and decent place of amusement on strict temperance lines. Her niece, Lilian Baylis, who had started her career as a child prodigy violinist in South Africa, joined her in this enterprise and took over the management in 1898. Under the direction of Charles Corri, a descendant of the Italian composer, Domenico Corri, who settled in Edinburgh in 1771, concerts were given, and in 1900

175

the first opera was produced – *The Bohemian Girl*. Corri was a musician who united ambition and humility in strange combination; he had not more than about sixteen or eighteen instruments at his disposal, but he took endless trouble to re-score the well-known operas for this modest band, and the result was that it never sounded like a makeshift. The Old Vic eventually achieved a high reputation as the 'home of Shakespeare'; it was the only theatre in the country where every one of Shakespeare's plays was produced in turn, even the most unfamiliar ones. The modern reader will here need reminding that in the latter part of the nineteenth century Shakespeare, apart from the spectacular productions of Irving and Beerbohm Tree, in which single plays were put on at enormous expense for a run, was hardly to be seen at all in England, and a dictum ascribed to Macready was commonly repeated – 'Shakespeare spells ruin!'

But all this time opera was being steadily built up at the Old Vic, where performances were given regularly on Thursdays and Saturdays, with occasional Saturday matinées. A large repertory was, of course, out of the question, but although *The Bohemian Girl* and *Maritana* were the stock favourites, along with *The Lily of Killarney* (Benedict) for St Patrick's Day (the Irish population of Lambeth always expected it), Corri was determined to raise the whole level of the opera, and Miss Baylis whole-heartedly supported him, as far as finances permitted. Corri's great ambition was to produce *Tristan and Isolde*, and he achieved it; he had re-scored the opera for a tiny orchestra with real artistic skill, and he had been obliged to make several cuts in order to bring the work within Miss Baylis's unbending limits of time – three hours, including intervals – but it was *Tristan* for all that, and no one who heard it could have left the theatre without a deep sense of respect both for Corri's idealism and for his practical accomplishment.

Miss Baylis always used to say that she was an ignorant woman, but she was a good judge of a singer and a judge of human nature, too. Her most marvellous gift was something quite indefinable, the quality that made everybody devoted to her and devoted to the theatre which she controlled. After the war was over the new interest in opera began to bear fruit at

176

the Old Vic, and Miss Baylis thought that the time had come to put *The Marriage of Figaro* on the stage again. It was not a new opera to the Vic, but it was many years since it had been seen there, and with a well-rehearsed ensemble it became such a success that it has been indispensable to the repertory every year. The revival of *Figaro* revealed that among the frequenters of the sixpenny gallery there was far more knowledge of music than most people might have expected. Conversations at the stage door with groups of enthusiasts who were waiting to offer two pennyworth of chrysanthemums to an adored *prima donna* were illuminating. 'Can't you give us *Don Giovanni* and *Così fan Tutte*? and what about *Norma*?' The gallery it seemed, possessed a long-standing subterranean tradition of old Italian opera going back to early Victorian days. *Don Giovanni* was put on the next year and received with immense enthusiasm; *Così fan Tutte* came later, but did not achieve the popularity of *The Magic Flute*. In all these operas success was due not to star singers, but to clever production and unselfish ensemble. The Old Vic was beginning to create an English operatic style of its own.

It was in January, 1931, that Sadler's Wells was opened as an 'Old Vic' for North London. Someone said to Miss Baylis, 'Then I suppose you'll be having opera every night of the week now, either at one theatre or the other.' (It had been decided that drama and opera were to be given at each theatre in alternate weeks.) Miss Baylis looked rather blank, and after a moment's reflection said, 'Yes, I suppose we shall', as if it had never occurred to her before. At that moment she was in fact utterly unprepared for the increase of work in the opera department, and had not realized that it would involve an increase of musical staff. It also involved an increase in the numbers of the orchestra, and she was greatly perturbed at the expense. The system of alternate weeks, or even alternate months of opera and drama at each theatre proved hopelessly unworkable, and although Miss Baylis was genuinely distressed at taking opera away from the Old Vic, where, as she insisted, opera, and not drama, had been the beginning of the theatre's new life, she felt obliged to accept the situation, and Sadler's Wells became the home of opera and ballet alone.

CHAPTER TWELVE

OPERA IN ENGLAND – THE IDEALISTS –
RUTLAND BOUGHTON – AMATEUR OPERA –
ENGLISH REPERTORY –
ETHEL SMYTH AND VAUGHAN WILLIAMS

THE history of all opera resolves itself into the conflict between
commercialism and idealism, and if English opera today is on
the way to establish itself on a firm footing, it is largely thanks
to the initiative and courage of the idealists. First and foremost
among these is Rutland Boughton (b. 1878), who in 1914
established an operatic centre at Glastonbury in the far west
of England. It was commonly said that his main object was to
create an English Bayreuth for the performance of his own
operas, and some colour was given to this allegation by the
fact that he composed and produced there a series of operas
dealing with the story of King Arthur and the Round Table.
The war interfered with these activities, but they were resumed
in 1919, and it then became evident that Boughton's own works
were only part of a much more comprehensive scheme. The
Glastonbury festivals were of the most modest description.
The theatre was a diminutive village hall, the orchestra a
grand pianoforte and not a very good one at that; the performers were many of them amateurs. The whole atmosphere
was that of an opera school rather than a festival to attract
strangers and make money. Old English opera was represented
by *Cupid and Death, Venus and Adonis* and *Dido and Aeneas.*
Boughton's own contributions were some of the Arthurian
operas and *The Immortal Hour* (1914). A Christmas mystery
opera, *Bethlehem*, was produced in 1916. It was hard to form
an adequate judgement of the Arthurian operas when produced under such hampering conditions, yet those very limitations led to suggestive experiments, such as the use of 'human
scenery'. *The Birth of Arthur* opened with a scene representing
a castle by the sea; the castle was a body of tenors and basses

178

architecturally grouped, and the ladies of the chorus executed formal movements at their feet to suggest waves. As they were all singing a prologue to the opera the general effect was by no means so ludicrous as it sounds in description, for Boughton is a great master of choral writing, and indeed his most original and impressive work is to be found in choral episodes. It was part of his operatic theory that the chorus should play a very important part in English opera; it was the tradition of Purcell, and it was acknowledged by everybody that choral singing is the form of music in which the English excel.

The Immortal Hour can hardly be said to have passed into the standard repertory, but it has achieved a unique position in our operatic life, for it has been revived several times by itself for runs of some duration, and has always attracted an increasing number of devotees. I use the word devotees with deliberate intention, for this is one of those rare operas to which an inward surrender has to be made. It could be analysed and subjected to criticism; it has many faults of style and technique. But over and over again musicians have gone to hear it in a critical spirit and have found themselves obliged to accept it against their wills. The reason is nothing occult; it is simply that the composer's inmost thought is always expressed in the vocal parts. The opera has been called Wagnerian; one might apply the same adjective to *Ivanhoe* because of its incongruous reminiscences of *Lohengrin* and *Tristan*. Boughton's opera is so un-Wagnerian that it might almost claim affinity with *Pelléas et Mélisande*; it shares with that work its misty romance, and its ingenious use of rhythm that quickens or slackens according to the emotion of the moment. Its characters belong to so remote a fairyland that if we had only the words to read we could hardly visualize them in human form; Boughton's music brings them so vividly before us that they become intensely vital to our imaginations, while we forget their corporeal reality.

Oxford and Cambridge were naturally places where musical idealism might find expression in opera. Stanford made a start with Gluck's *Orpheus* at Cambridge as far back as 1892; Oxford performed *Fidelio* in 1909, and the Cambridge performance of *The Magic Flute* in 1911 was what led to the immense popularity which that opera now enjoys in England.

In more recent years Oxford has shown how to combine learning with imagination in the revivals of Monteverdi's *Orpheus* and *The Coronation of Poppea,* while Cambridge encouraged the cult of Purcell by staging *King Arthur* and *The Fairy Queen.* For many years the Misses Radford have organized convincing performances of many 'museum operas' at Falmouth and have shown them to possess a great deal more life than the musical historians have credited them with. The Glasgow Grand Opera Society, consisting mainly of amateurs, and conducted by Dr Erik Chisholm, has within the last few years given the first performance in Great Britain of Mozart's *Idomeneo* and Berlioz's *The Trojans;* it has also revived his *Benvenuto Cellini* and *Béatrice et Bénédict.*

All these operas have been given in English, and in every case it was found necessary to get a new English translation made. There are still some connoisseurs who maintain that it is sacrilege to perform any opera except in the language in which it was originally written. Sometimes this attitude is due merely to exclusiveness, to pride in their own exaggerated critical sense for vocal technique, or in their intimate knowledge of foreign languages. Still, the position is a logical one, and if consistently maintained would forbid all translation of literary works. This doctrine is often held jointly with another of long standing – that the English language is unmusical and unsuited for singing. The curious thing is that whereas this objection to opera in English is of very long standing, and goes back to the period of Queen Anne, there does not seem to have been any sign of its application to oratorio, apart from a little squabbling between a few critics and singers over the Passion music of J. S. Bach. It is waste of time to bring forward arguments in support of the musicality of English; either they fall on deaf ears, or one is preaching to the converted. The most sensible way to look at the matter is to acknowledge the fact that English is the language of this country and that therefore we must either have opera in English or renounce all hope of understanding it, for it needs a very close knowledge of a foreign language to be able to follow it when sung on the stage. Mr Cecil Forsyth, in his illuminating and amusing book, *Music and Nationalism,* first published in 1911, suggested that it would be a good thing if all the foreign operatic stars were compelled to sing in English as a condition of being engaged at Covent Garden. Their varieties of accent might be even more diverting than the varieties of Italian or German that have been heard already with a cast of mixed nationalities.

Operatic translations have been a standing joke for many years, and their literary level is no better in other countries than it is here. But English is a very elastic language, and its rhythms are so varied that it can be fitted to the music of any other nationality – with one proviso, that the original language has been respected by the composer and not distorted for the sake of singers' effects. The chief difficulty is that most syllables in English are short, especially when strongly accented, so that there is a very limited choice of words suitable to be placed on long-drawn-out notes. The older composers did not trouble much over this; even Sullivan (in *Ivanhoe*) is careless in the prolongation of short syllables. The present age expects a higher standard of English declamation, and that is another reason why most of the accepted operatic translations ought to be revised. The only trouble is that singers are very reluctant to learn the new ones. If a singer has learned one version of an opera it is a matter of very serious difficulty to learn another in the same language, and in performance the slightest hesitation or nervousness may send him back to the old version for the rest of the scene. Some singers, I fancy, really prefer 'operatic English'; it is what they are accustomed to, and they sometimes seem suddenly embarrassed when they realize, perhaps in the course of a performance, that what they are singing is sense, and imperatively demands a sensible interpretation.

All this comes from the inherent falsity of opera, if we judge opera by the majority of those which form the standard repertory. Some people have maintained that opera should deal only with the world of magic and fantasy; that was the view of Peri and Monteverdi, of Gluck and Wagner. The general public has not accepted mythological opera with any great cordiality; it presupposes an elect audience of persons who have had the advantages of a classical education. Ordinary mortals are more interested in heroes, and even when the subject is heroic, they prefer it to come within appreciable distance of their own time. There is also the approach to opera from the other end – the comic play with songs interspersed. In this case everything must be of the present day; the period may be anything the costumier likes, but the characters will talk the language of today, and the fact that they sing will make them all the more comic.

Now consider how this affects the composer and the singer. We are accustomed to think that music may be comic, sentimental or serious, as the case may be; but take away the words and the stage situation, and it is often impossible to say what the character of the music is. The music is, as Mendelssohn said, *itself*; it is not to be summed up in any of these conventional adjectives. It is easy to see how a composer who is sincerely interested in his own processes of composition is inclined to make every number of his comic operas more and more serious, as long as the words do not insist on treatment that is definitely farcical or grotesque. This reacts on the singer, all the more so as singers take their own voices very seriously indeed.

We have further to take into account the fact that the public, in general, is more interested in singers than in composers. There are two ways in which the public can show that it has been moved; one is by applause and the other is by silence. Those moments of silence at the end of a performance are rare experiences; it is seldom that a singer or a composer can bring an audience to the condition of being too much overcome to want to applaud. Applause, in fact, is not really a sign that the audience is inwardly moved; it almost always means admiration for the performance of a difficult task. And once this habit of applauding performance – performance in the sense that a tight-rope act or an athletic feat is a 'performance' – is accepted, audiences go to the theatre not to see plays and operas, but to see individual actors and singers. This will probably seem perfectly natural to many of my readers, and those who consider themselves men of the world and persons of taste will no doubt say that I am like a child going to the theatre for the first time, if I am more interested in Hamlet himself than in the celebrated actor who is representing him.

We must indeed be grateful for the existence of the 'immortal classics'; for they are the only plays and operas that we can bear to see over and over again merely for the sake of

182

comparing fresh interpretations of them. For when it comes to average modern works, we may perhaps want to see our particular favourite in all his or her different roles, but we do not want to see the same indifferent work a dozen times for the sake of comparing different individuals. We may well pity the unfortunate critic who has to attend some four or five performances of *La Bohème* within a fortnight, merely because there is a new Mimi in each.

It is this exaggerated interest in the individual artist that has caused composers to write operas that give him opportunities for display. As they have been doing this for three hundred years they are not likely to stop doing it now. And what English audiences have wanted from their singers was the kind of noise that the Italians made; either the real thing at great expense, or for ordinary people a cheaper home-grown imitation. That is the reason why Balfe and Wallace, with the literary assistance of Bunn and Fitzball, wrote the romantic operas which are at one and the same time the laughing-stock and the delight of the British public. They are the operas which our singers love to sing, and that is why the language of Bunn is the language in which they feel most at home.

It is observable that the connoisseurs who have such high standards of singing are always far more deeply concerned about the performance of Verdi and Donizetti than they would be about that of Gluck and Mozart. With the earlier operas they might even tolerate a translation, and think well of it if it was adroit enough to make someone say that 'it sounded as if the great master had composed his music to the English words'. That could never be allowed in the case of Verdi, apart from *Falstaff*, which stands by itself. Make *Trovatore* sound like an English opera? An unthinkable sacrilege. The reason is this – that Gluck and Mozart demand intelligence, dramatic understanding and a constant sense of the word and its significance, whereas the early Verdi and all the operas of that period required little more than fine voices. We must not underrate the value of a really beautiful human voice. That value has only too often been expressed in terms of money, as if money was all that mattered; what does matter, whether the singer is paid or not, is the appeal to the human heart, and it is an appeal that is universal – it belongs to the gallery as well as to the boxes. It is for that reason that we are bound to recall Melba and Tetrazzini with unfeigned gratitude and admiration, and those who heard them can understand the raptures of their elders over Grisi and Mario, or Pasta and Rubini.

Is it possible for English singers to sing in real English and achieve such results as these? The question has often been asked, and it is generally answered in too much of a hurry. The singers exist, and have always existed; there can be no doubt about that. The real question is whether it is possible to sing beautifully in English. I am not competent to discuss this from the point of view of a singer or a singing-master, and it involves technicalities which would be out of place in this book. All I want to do here is to draw the reader's serious attention to the problem, and ask him to thrash it out with his own conscience, whether he really wants to hear English words sung with a proper pronunciation and at the same time with pure beauty of vocal tone. It is a rare experience, but if the musical public insisted on it, it would become commoner and might even set up a normal standard of what English singing ought to be.

If we could establish that normal standard, it might make a great difference in the attitude of the British public towards opera. It has been said that we are not an opera-loving nation; I suspect the writers who maintain this view. Most of them, if they are not of the small tribe of connoisseurs who will listen to opera only at Milan and Vienna, are at heart puritans still haunted by a sense of sin whenever they hear *Don Giovanni* or *La Traviata*. They are trying to wile us away from these vain delights to what Charles Lamb called 'that profanation of the cheerful playhouse' – the oratorio, though they would be horrified to think that oratorios had ever been presented within the profane walls of a theatre. The box-office receipts of Sadler's Wells are a truer guide, and they tell us quite plainly that the interest in opera is steadily increasing.

As regards repertory, we are still more or less in the same situation as the German opera houses were a hundred years ago, when native opera and opera in the native language were

184

making a brave struggle against the competition of the Italian opera established by the court. The analogy is not strictly exact, because international opera, either at the King's Theatre in the Haymarket or at Covent Garden, has never been financed out of the royal purse. Nor has it ever had to submit to so much royal interference as the court operas of Munich or Berlin. Since the end of the last war (1945) a new management has taken over Covent Garden Theatre and established a company consisting mainly of native singers, singing all operas (apart from occasional guest performances) in English. Both Covent Garden and Sadler's Wells are now receiving regular subsidies from the Government through the Arts Council, and it is to be hoped that the old international seasons will never be revived again. In former days Covent Garden gave opera in foreign languages for a wealthy and socially exclusive audience while the Old Vic and Sadler's Wells gave opera in English for the poor. There are still a few people, not merely remnants of the older generation, but younger enthusiasts as well, haunted by a snobbish nostalgia for the supposed glamour of the Victorian age, who do their best to make propaganda for a return to the old system, but I hope that the majority of my readers will agree with me in thinking that we must frankly accept the economic conditions of today which are tending to make both Covent Garden and Sadler's Wells opera houses for the people in general, as has now happened with practically all the opera houses in Europe, whatever the situation may still be on the American continents. We have the opportunity now to make these two London theatres worthy parallels to the Opéra and the Opéra-Comique in Paris, both equal in artistic and social status and dividing the repertory without rivalry or competition, but solely on grounds of size, spectacular operas being given at the large house and more intimate ones at the smaller. At both theatres, as in Paris, it should be indispensable that all operas be performed in the language of the audience.

Paris has for centuries enjoyed the advantage of an enormous repertory of operas composed for Paris to French words; even though the composers, from Lully to Meyerbeer at any rate, have often been foreigners by birth, they have become French by adoption. Here in England we have suffered so long from the foreign domination of opera that it is only natural that the British public should take comparatively little interest in British operas. There are so few chances, even now, of seeing them anywhere that it is not surprising if opera-lovers who are not students of musical history should be ignorant of their names. Let us try to make up a list of native operas which might, in more favourable circumstances, be reasonably included in the repertory of a British opera house. Naturally, it is not suggested that our two opera houses should at once put all of them into the coming season; even with a State-supported opera on the scale of Paris, one could not expect to hear all of them every year.

I should like to begin with three operas of Purcell – *Dido and Aeneas, King Arthur,* and *The Fairy Queen*. It is a pity that these three works should be relegated to the category of 'museum operas', for that means that they are never performed except by amateurs under conditions which inevitably demand that allowances should be made for some shortcoming or other. It is possible, in spite of shortcomings, to derive an impression of poetry and beauty from such performances, as the Monteverdi operas at Oxford showed; but all the same one could wish that these historic masterpieces might be put on the stage in such a way that nobody need feel anxieties. There can be no question about the dramatic power of these three works of Purcell; they have been seen at any rate often enough to provide proof of their being completely convincing in actual performance. The main difficulty about *Dido* is that it was designed for a very small theatre (and this applies equally to *Venus and Adonis*, which, although more of a 'museum piece', is still beautiful on the stage); and even in a house the size of Sadler's Wells it calls for exceptional ingenuity of treatment. The other two operas of Purcell need the cooperation of a large dramatic cast, as well as a good deal of spectacular effect; it might be more effective to revive them at Covent Garden than at Sadler's Wells. Purcell is for us what Rameau is for the French – and indeed a Rameau opera on the stage has much more affinity with Purcell than with Handel; the stage of the present Paris Opéra is far too large for Rameau, but that has not prevented his being revived there with considerable success, and Rameau now

186

belongs to the standard French repertory just as much as Gluck.

Handel belongs more to the museum category. He cannot be claimed as a native of these islands, and his operas were all written to Italian words, so that it is difficult to make out a case for including him in a national British repertory. Some of his oratorios have been put on the stage at Cambridge with considerable success, but it may be doubted whether a theatre is a practically convenient place for them, although *Susanna*, in a rather abridged form, has recently been made quite effective. *Susanna,* as Handel's friend Lady Shaftesbury observed, is actually in the style of a comic opera.

But even if we exclude Handel, *The Beggar's Opera* ought to have a permanent place in our repertory, all the more since Benjamin Britten's new version has adapted it very successfully to the modern stage. After *The Beggar's Opera* we shall have to make a long jump. Arne and Dibdin may be resuscitated for special performances and special conditions; but I can think of nothing in the 'ballad opera' period that could be taken into the regular repertory.

Weber's *Oberon* undoubtedly claims a place there. The libretto is as English as it can be in its absurdities, and the whole plan of the opera reminds us more of *King Arthur* than of any continental opera. It was composed for England and to us it belongs; but it must be given with its funny old English spoken dialogue, not with any of the various recitatives added by other German composers after Weber's death. It is true that Weber himself had hoped to be able to rearrange it for the German stage; but failing the work of Weber's own brain, it is better for the English stage as it is. It is well suited to a theatre of the size of Sadler's Wells, for in a large house – it was revived in 1938 at Rome – it needs a great display of scenery and supers, and the music then seems a little small for it all.

From Weber we pass to the three old favourites, *The Bohemian Girl, Maritana* and *The Lily of Killarney*. If we wash their faces, will there be anything left of them? After the opening of Sadler's Wells, Miss Baylis, who had a very tender affection for these three operas, after having lived with them for thirty years, was heard to say rather sadly that she didn't think she would ever dare to put them on the stage again. In the new theatre, with new conditions of production and a new standard of orchestral playing, the tattered gipsy maiden might have felt the marble halls to be less home-like than she had anticipated. I have often wondered whether *The Bohemian Girl* (or the other two, very likely) has ever been properly rehearsed, or even rehearsed at all, since the first production in 1843. It was taken round the country by travelling companies with no time to spare for the old stock works; everybody was supposed to know it by heart, with all its traditional business, the accumulation of years and years. If a new singer had to take part in it for the first time, she was generally pushed on without a rehearsal of any kind. There is nothing in the least unusual in this country about operas being performed without any rehearsal whatever; it has happened even at Covent Garden, though it is not the habitual practice at Sadler's Wells. The public may not be aware of this fact, but any opera singer will confirm the truth of it. After all, why should an opera be rehearsed when everybody has sung in it before? English orchestras can read anything at sight; opera conductors are not drawn from those who have had an academic education, but from those who have played violin or violincello in a touring company. The stage business of an opera is a fixed tradition, and any way it does not amount to much. What would those old operas be like if they were subjected to a scholarly revision from the original manuscripts and earliest editions, and then rehearsed with as much 'loving reverence' as we all are supposed to put into Mozart and Beethoven? I wonder if the audiences would enjoy them as much as they did in the bad old days.

Ivanhoe has already been discussed. *Shamus O'Brien* might bear revival, though it really needs an almost entirely Irish cast. *Much Ado About Nothing* deserves consideration; *The Travelling Companion* is on its way to general acceptance. It has a good nucleus of steady supporters, and the singers all enjoy it; it will win its way in time, even if it drops out for a year now and then.

The revival of *The Wreckers* at Sadler's Wells in 1939 was a great tribute of affection to Ethel Smyth and a clear proof that the passage of thirty years had by no means made the work old-fashioned; it is still vital music and drama. Some of her other operas might well be revived, notably *The Bo'sun's Mate*, a comic opera in one act on a story by W. W. Jacobs.

The Tempest, by Nicholas Gatty (Surrey Theatre, 1920, and Old Vic, 1922), and *Macbeth*, by Lawrence Collingwood (Sadler's Wells, 1937), both stick closely to Shakespeare's text and are interesting musical illustrations of it; each has had some success on its first production.

Whether the operas of Frederick Delius can become part of the standard repertory may be doubted; but they ought all to be kept in mind and revived from time to time. *Koanga* was first produced in Germany (Elberfeld, 1904); it has a picturesque American background and is to some extent based on old slave songs which give it a character of its own. *A Village Romeo and Juliet* (Berlin, 1907) is founded on a story by the Swiss writer, Gottfried Keller; it is not very dramatic, but it has much beautiful music. *Fennimore and Gerda* (Frankfurt, 1919) has not yet been performed in this country.

Hugh the Drover, by Ralph Vaughan Williams (b. 1872), has already won the affections of the Sadler's Wells audience. It was composed as far back as 1911–14, but it was not performed until 1924, when it was brought out at the Royal College of Music and later taken up by the British National Opera Company. The composer calls it a 'romantic ballad opera'; the libretto, by Harold Child, deals with English country life in the time of the Napoleonic wars. The music is in the spirit of old English traditional melodies, though none are actually used complete; the popular attraction of the opera is a very realistic prize-fight in the course of the finale to the first act. As in Rutland Boughton's operas, there is a great deal of work for the chorus, in which the Sadler's Wells company has shown to great advantage. *Hugh the Drover* is a modern revival of the 'village opera' of the eighteenth century, but without its affectations and artificialities; it has a great deal of humour, but it is in the main a serious work, with a completely modern outlook on music and sometimes on life as well.

Sir John in Love (1929) is based on *The Merry Wives of Windsor*; it was revived at Sadler's Wells in 1945. A comic opera, *The Poisoned Kiss*, was produced at Cambridge in 1936 and repeated for one performance by the Cambridge company at Sadler's Wells. It was revived again by the students of the Royal Academy of Music for the composer's seventy-fifth birthday in 1947. *The Shepherds of the Delectable Mountains* (Bristol, 1926) is a short one-act opera of religious character based on an episode from *Pilgrim's Progress*; it was very successfully revived at Sadler's Wells in 1946. Another short opera by Vaughan Williams is *Riders to the Sea* (Royal College of Music, 1937, Cambridge, 1938), which ought certainly to find a place in our permanent repertory.

In the first edition of this book (1940) I wrote at this point: 'If a young English composer did succeed in making an immediate and sensational success at Sadler's Wells, where else can that opera be performed?' Five years later the unexpected actually happened. In 1945 *Peter Grimes*, the first opera of Benjamin Britten (b. 1913), to a libretto by Montagu Slater based on Crabbe's poem *The Borough*, was produced at Sadler's Wells, since when it has been performed at Basle, Zurich, Antwerp, Hamburg, Berlin, Milan, Stockholm and Copenhagen as well as at New York and elsewhere in America. At Budapest it is now a popular repertory work. In 1947 it was given a more spacious production at Covent Garden – it is an opera which imperatively needs a large theatre – and in 1948 the Covent Garden company were invited to perform it at Paris and Brussels. This was the first occasion on which an English opera company had ever appeared on the stages of the Opéra and the Monnaie. History records no first opera by any composer, except *Hänsel and Gretel*, which met with such an immediate and incontestable success, and no British composer except Balfe had ever achieved such a conquest of Europe. The box office success of *Peter Grimes* at both Sadler's Wells and Covent Garden leads one to hope that it will become a permanent repertory opera, and even one permanent repertory opera by a native composer, on an essentially native subject, too, means a definite encouragement to all other native composers to regard opera as a practical hope. When a modern English opera, and that, too, a work in the most uncompromisingly modern style, can stand up at the box office to *Carmen* and *Trovatore*, *Rosenkavalier* and *Turandot*, we may justly feel that a new chapter in English operatic history has really begun.

A grave problem is presented in this country by the training of opera singers, conductors and producers. The schools of music take their work seriously enough, but what is to became of all these operatic students when there is only one permanent opera house in the country? In other countries a beginner can find an opening in a small provincial theatre and gradually work his way up from one theatre to another; here, apart from the precarious work of the travelling companies, there is nothing. The touring companies are a good school of rough-and-ready practical training, but they cannot teach those artistic ideals which ought to be inculcated through subordinate work in an opera house of the first rank. We shall make little progress with opera in this country until opera houses with a resident company and a regular season's work are established in the great provincial centres. It could be done, if people would be content to begin on a small scale, and if municipalities would give some encouragement. But it is no good starting with 'heavyweight' operas like those of Wagner and Strauss; a public must be found for a repertory based mainly on the older comic operas, and singers must be trained who can not only sing these works, but act them, too.

Even before the outbreak of war in 1939 lamentations were heard in all countries over the ruin of opera, and it is perhaps a matter for surprise that under the conditions of the present day (1949) the operatic situation should give grounds for encouragement rather than for despair. The fact is that before the war opera was still being carried on in many countries on the assumption of a social system that was gradually becoming extinct. Opera was associated with wealth and grandeur; but the economic situation was rapidly making wealth and grandeur obsolete. The economic problem of opera was further aggravated by the rising demands of orchestral players. The conventional repertory, based largely on Wagner and Strauss, required enormous orchestras, and at this moment the cost of the orchestra is a disproportionately heavy burden on the operatic budget, and it is a disastrous obstacle to the achievement of high standards, because rehearsals have necessarily to be reduced to the absolute minimum. In this country we are faced with the further difficulty arising from the fact that a good orchestral player can earn a better living as a free-lance playing for cinema and gramophone recordings than by dedicating himself exclusively, or at least conscientiously, to the daily service of an opera house.

Contrary to all expectation, the economic ruin of Europe has not brought about the complete ruin of operatic activities. Even in Germany, where many theatres had been destroyed, opera was at once reorganized in makeshift buildings of all kinds long before the ordinary amenities and conveniences of civilization could be brought into anything like working order. In England and Holland, the least operatic of all countries, there is now observable a determined effort to establish national and popular opera on a permanent basis.

Each country has its own general repertory, though *Carmen, Cavalleria* and *Pagliacci* may be common to all of them. England is less chauvinistic in music than any country in the world, and we are ready to appreciate foreign operas of many different types. But for a practical working repertory we must gradually choose out those which really suit our own English style; we cannot do everything, and it is better to limit ourselves to what we can do best. The choice will be determined by the qualities of English voices and the English language. Both are predominantly light and agile in character; they are admirably suited to old-fashioned comic opera like that of Mozart, Rossini and Auber. They will sound equally well in *Faust* and *Carmen*; in the heavier Italian operas such as *Aïda* and *Otello* we must simply accept a vocally lighter interpretation all round than Italians would give. *Falstaff* is admirably suited to an English company, indeed perhaps better than to Italians, who do not much enjoy ensemble singing.

An officially subsidized opera house can justify its existence only if it maintains artistic standards far above those of the ordinary commercial theatre, both in choice of repertory and in details of execution. It would be premature at present to apply to this country the conditions, which in some others are imposed by law, as to the production every year of a fixed minimum of new operas by native composers; we would rather hope that such legal obligations would never be necessary, because the public itself would demand such productions and support them as a matter of course. The main thing is that in every town where there is a subsidized opera house that

192

theatre should be the central focus of all musical activities, the leading musical institution, to which it is taken for granted that all the most accomplished artists, in every department, singers, orchestra and invisible staff, too, naturally belong and make it their pride to belong. It is only when such corporate unity on the stage has been firmly established that a corporate public can be built up for it and a sense of spiritual communion created between the auditorium and the stage. Such a sense has indeed been achieved, if only rarely, at certain times and in certain places; Monteverdi may have known it at Mantua, Wagner certainly realized it at Bayreuth, and so, in her own humble way, did Lilian Baylis at the Old Vic. But it cannot be based on the adoration of individual singers; our adoration must be for the work itself. Nor need it by any means be invariably a devout adoration; we need comedy no less than tragedy, and corporate adoration is none the worse for being hilarious.

These suggestions will not meet with the approval of the perfectionists who profess such exalted standards that they cannot bear to listen to any opera except in its original language. Their attitude is theoretically logical, but to carry out their principles in practice would need – in a permanent opera house – at least five separate companies of five different nationalities, English, French, German, Italian and Russian, and we may pity the unfortunate manager who was responsible for keeping them all in order. I should have more respect for the perfectionists if they really lived up to their creed; but whereas a Welsh accent in an English opera will set their teeth on edge, they will accept the thickest German accent in an Italian opera without noticing it in the least. As long as the conductor and principals have foreign names and the performance is not in English, that is generally enough for them. They are in most cases slaves of the wireless and the gramophone, utterly oblivious to the falsification of tone values inseparable from these mechanical inventions.

An opera that is heard but not seen, whether by gramophone, wireless or in concert performance, is not an opera at all. If we have seen it often before on the stage, we may be able to reconstruct it in imagination – as far as the inevitable mutilations will allow – just as we may listen to *Petrouchka* at a concert and recall the ballet; but to hear an unknown opera without seeing it is almost as useless as it would be to see an opera without being able to hear a note of it. Opera is drama, a thing done, acted and seen; and history shows that whenever music has sought to tyrannize completely over drama it has been the ruin of opera. It may be asked why it is, then, that many people derive pleasure from opera without taking the slightest interest in its dramatic aspect; the answer probably is that they enjoy the exaggeration of personality in a singer, and an over-emotional style of singing which serious concert-goers, including oratorio-lovers, would feel to be repulsive. Commercial opera has, of course, always exploited this desire, and on the whole it has been the ruin of artistic singing. The history of the theatre, both poetical and musical, has shown from time immemorial the eternal conflict between the actor or singer and the poet or composer; one might think that it was the duty of producers and conductors to defend the cause of the latter, but in modern times they have often been more inclined to impose their own private tyranny on both parties. Shakespeare and Purcell have had a good deal to put up with since they died; but they still survive.

BIBLIOGRAPHY

GENERAL

R. A. STREATFEILD. *The Opera: A Sketch of the Development of Opera, with full Descriptions of all Works in the Modern Repertory.* London: George Routledge & Sons, 1925.

EDWARD J. DENT. *Foundations of English Opera: A Study of Musical Drama in England during the Seventeenth Century.* Cambridge University Press, 1928.

CECIL FORSYTH. *Music and Nationalism: A Study of English Opera.* London: Macmillan & Co, 1915.

ERNEST WALKER. *A History of Music in England.* Oxford: Clarendon Press, 1907.

FRANK HOWES and PHILIP HOPE-WALLACE. *A Key to Opera.* London: Blackie & Son, 1939.

D. J. GROUT. *A Short History of Opera.* New York: Columbia University Press, 1947.

SINGLE COMPOSERS

HENRY PRUNIÈRES. *Monteverdi: His Life and Work.* London: J. M. Dent & Sons, 1926.

J. A. WESTRUP. *Purcell.* London: J. M. Dent & Sons, 1937.

R. A. STREATFEILD. *Handel.* London: Methuen & Co, 1909.

MARTIN COOPER. *Gluck.* London: Chatto & Windus, 1935.

ALFRED EINSTEIN. *Gluck.* London: J. M. Dent & Sons, 1936.

ERNEST NEWMAN. *Gluck and the Opera: A Study in Musical History.* London: Bertram Dobell, 1895.

EDWARD J. DENT. *Mozart's Operas: A Critical Study.* London: Chatto & Windus, 1913.

DYNELEY HUSSEY. *Wolfgang Amadé Mozart.* London: Kegan Paul, Trench, Trubner & Co, 1928.

FRANCIS TOYE. *Rossini: A Study in Tragi-comedy.* London: William Heinemann, 1934.

F. BONAVIA. *Verdi.* Oxford University Press, 1930.

FRANCIS TOYE. *Giuseppe Verdi: His Life and Works.* London: William Heinemann, 1931.

W. H. HADOW. *Richard Wagner*. London: Thornton Butterworth, 1934.

ERNEST NEWMAN. *The Life of Richard Wagner*. London: Cassell & Co, 1933.

G. BERNARD SHAW. *The Perfect Wagnerite*. London: Grant Richards, 1898.

MARTIN COOPER. *Georges Bizet*. London: Oxford University Press, 1938.

D. C. PARKER. *Georges Bizet: His Life and Works*. London: Kegan Paul, Trench, Trubner & Co, 1926.

WINTON DEAN. *Bizet*. London: J. M. Dent & Sons, 1948.

DYNELEY HUSSEY. *Verdi*. London: J. M. Dent & Sons, 1940.

INDEX

Morgan, Lady, 87
Moses in Egypt (Rossini), 66
Mountain Sylph, The (Barnett), 169–70
Mount Edgcumbe, Earl of, 64
Moussorgsky, Modeste, 100
Mozart, W. A., 68, 107, 183; early operas, 51; *Idomeneo*, 49, 69, 110, 115, 180; *Seraglio*, 51, 110; *Marriage of Figaro*, 51–4, 87, 107, 133, 139, 177; *Don Giovanni*, 51–2, 54–5, 107; *Così fan Tutte*, 51, 52, 55–6, 107, 109; *Clemenza di Tito*, 56, 111; *Magic Flute*, 56, 138, 179
Much Ado About Nothing (Shakespeare), 94, 188
Much Ado About Nothing (Stanford, 173
Music associated with magic and religion, 19, 81, 82
Mussolini, 145

Nabucco (Verdi), 86
Naples, opera at, 24–5, 34, 35, 39
Napoleon I, Emperor, 52, 59
Neues vom Tage (Hindemith), 143
Nicolini, 132, 165
Norma (Bellini), 65–6
Noverre, J. G., 131, 135

Oberon (Weber), 51, 69, 169, 187
Offenbach, Jacques, 46 note, 69
Old Vic Theatre, 175ff., 185
Opera, attitude of English towards, 13ff., 28–30, 80, 83, 183–4; history of, 18ff.; influence of Wagner on, 15–16; conventions of, 16ff., 111
Opera semi-seria, 62, 65
Operetta, 95
Orchestra, 21, 40, 52, 70; in

Verdi and Wagner, 92; in earliest operas, 101ff.; in romantic operas, 111–12; Wagner, 112ff.; Strauss, 137, 138; Dorset Garden Theatre, 155
Orfeo (Gluck), 44–5, 46, 47, 110
Orfeo (Monteverdi), 32, 102, 119
Orfeo (Poliziano), 30
Organ on the stage, 67
Orsèolo (Pizzetti), 144–5
Ossian ou les Bardes (Lesueur), 59
Otello (Rossini), 125–6
Otello (Verdi), 91–3, 114
Overture, function of, 23–4, 75
Oxford, opera at, 32, 180, 186

Paer, Ferdinando, 60, 64, 71, 89, 109, 112
Pagliacci (Leoncavallo), 97, 145
Paisiello, Giovanni, 52, 53, 60
Palestrina (Pfitzner), 140
Pariati, Pietro, 125
Paride ed Elena (Gluck), 46
Paris, opera in, 34–5, 46, 57f., 62, 66–8, 79, 81, 89, 93f., 95, 96, 185
Paris: Opéra, 13, 41, 96, 185; Opéra-Comique, 41, 185
Parodies of opera, 154–5
Parsifal (Wagner), 75, 77, 78, 81f., 127, 128, 129, 140
Pasta, Madame, 87, 184
Pasticcio operas, 165, 169
Pastor Fido, Il (Handel), 18 note
Patti, Adelina, 55
Pelléas et Mélisande (Debussy), 140–1
Pepusch, Dr, 167
Pepys, Samuel, 31, 155, 162
'Perfectionists', attitude of, 193
Pergolesi, G. B., 25, 95
Peri, Jacopo, 30, 33, 101, 104, 181
Peter Grimes (Britten), 190
Pfitzner, Hans, 140

203